D0469404

"Kathleen Chesto offers us a meaningful lo[...] through nostalgic formula prayers of ea[...] temporary updates. More, she calls us to th[...] own words of conversation with God. These are great individual rituals.

"This book should be on the family prayer stand, the coffee table, anywhere it cannot be forgotten. The language will invite any parent, child, and even families without children to use and enjoy it often. Keep this book where it will become dog-eared with use!"

Leo T. Bistak, Deacon
Continuing Formation and Evangelization
Diocese of Toledo

"Kathleen Chesto's *Family Prayers for Family Times* is an excellent resource for the Catholic family. It presents a starting point for families just learning to pray and gives new ideas for those with more prayer experience.

"She helps families to recognize and celebrate the many ways that God is working in their lives. Many of the prayers and rituals are centered around the family meal. Chesto recognizes the sacredness of the family table and uses it as an opportunity to build and celebrate the community of the family. This book of prayers will help parents to highlight both the ordinary events and the milestones in their family life."

Kay and Gary Atchison
Executive Directors
Christian Family Movement

"From short blessings and prayers to more detailed rituals for family occasions, this book is a treasure. It includes rituals for traditional holidays, as well as prayers for times of anger or need, blessing a new home, getting engaged, or grieving over death. Except for traditional prayers, most of the language seems to move toward inclusivity. A very helpful book for families interested in making prayer an important part of their lives."

Arlene Goetze
Catholic Women's Network

"Rituals introduce us to and encourage us in the practice of finding God in all things. Kathleen Chesto's *Family Prayer for Family Times* is a wise and tender book of rituals and prayers for people struggling to find God in the ordinariness of family life. Chesto has a knack not only for choosing prayers that are apt and lovely in their simplicity, but for helping us see the sacred dimension in all that we as families do—from bringing the baby home, to losing the first tooth, to sending a child to college, to seeking forgiveness for the ways we hurt one another."

Wendy M. Wright
Author, *Sacred Dwelling: A Spirituality of Family Life*
Associate Professor of Theology
Creighton University

"Responding to the reality of the presence of God in all our varied moments is the task of a lifetime, one in which even the most practiced of pray-ers needs encouragement. Kathleen Chesto's book really gives us a hand, no matter how much or how little skill we have. She is clearly seasoned in the business of family living, and a real artist at designing prayer moments. She has gleaned for home use some of the best of the tradition as well as suggesting many very creative new ideas. There are prayers and rituals that can be used as they are or adapted easily.

"Avoiding pious jargon, Chesto offers words and activities that one could imagine ordinary people (like our own families) actually using. Communicated through her engaging, down-to-earth style, her encouragement is the greatest gift of all. This book is a real support for the praying together that we have long said is needed to help us stay together lovingly."

Pat Livingston, counselor, speaker
Author, *Lessons of the Heart*

"In this collection of traditions, celebrations, and rituals, the author draws on her twenty-five years of married life to offer a blend of Catholic tradition and practical suggestions for developing a sense of God's presence in all family activities: the first day of school, learning to ride a bike, and so forth."

James J. Higgins, C.SS.R.
Liguorian Magazine

Family Prayer for Family Times

Traditions, Celebrations, and Rituals

KATHLEEN O'CONNELL CHESTO

TWENTY-THIRD PUBLICATIONS
BAYARD 🔵 Mystic, CT 06355

DEDICATION

To all those children who have touched my life
with their awareness of God
and their hunger for prayer
particularly Jon, Becky, and Liz.

Scripture quotations are from the *New Revised Standard Version Bible*, © 1989, by the Division of Christian Education of the National Council of the Churches of Christ in the United States of America. Published by Thomas Nelson, Inc., Nashville, TN.

Excerpts from the English translation of The Roman Missal, © 1973, International Committee on English in the Liturgy, Inc. (ICEL). All rights reserved.

Seventh printing 2006

Twenty-Third Publications/Bayard
185 Willow Street
P.O. Box 180
Mystic, CT 06355
(860) 536-2611
(800) 321-0411

ISBN 0-89622-668-9
Library of Congress Catalog Card Number 95-78537
Printed in the U.S.A.

PREFACE

In preparing this text, I have relied heavily on the opinions and experiences of my own young adult children and the families who have been part of our spiritual journey. Some of the rituals and prayers reflect our family life, some reflect theirs. Special thanks is due to the small group of children who supported this work by learning and using some of the prayers: Peter, Sarah Lynn, Kaitlyn, and Carolyn Aiksnoras, Kaitlyn and Kenny Cadoret, Annie and John Giammatteo, and Brian and Caitlin O'Dea. Special thanks to their parents and to all the parents I have met throughout the country who have encouraged and assisted me by voicing their needs.

Throughout the text, I have tried to use inclusive language. This became difficult in some of the more traditional blessings and prayers, and some of the psalms. Consequently, some of these still retain their masculine language for God.

In the prayers and rituals, the use of he (she) became cumbersome, and I simply alternated using different pronouns for different prayers. I am confident that families who use these prayers and rituals will feel comfortable translating the gender to what is appropriate to their circumstances. This is true for the directions to the prayers and rituals, as well; please adapt them to whatever applies in your own household.

TABLE OF CONTENTS

INTRODUCTION

I grew up in the 1950s, the era of the family rosary crusade, when Fr. Patrick Peyton assured us that "the family that prayed together, stayed together." As Catholics, we had been instructed to pray the rosary daily for the conversion of Russia. In our house this meant that every evening after supper we went to the living room, knelt down on the wooden floor, and leaned on a chair in front of us to say the rosary.

I don't remember these prayer times as happy, or even particularly prayerful, only as somewhat long and painful. Yet the rosary offered my family a way to begin to pray together, something that would have been quite difficult for us without this evening ritual. (And we as a family have managed to "stay together," so there may be something to be said for the motto.)

Our home was filled with other, less complicated rituals. There were holy water fonts by the doors and we blessed ourselves on entering and leaving. We made May altars in the spring, and decorated a crèche in Advent. We knelt by our beds each evening to recite a few simple rote prayers, to ask God to forgive our faults, to pray for our needs, and to ask God to bless our family and friends. And there were the more complicated church rituals of novenas, stations of the cross, and processions.

Rituals are a safe way to pray. They follow a format. Participants can know what to expect and what is expected of them. People who are a little uncomfortable with the idea of spontaneous prayer—that is, prayer we "create" on the spot, expressing our own thoughts and using our own words—find rituals comforting. I am sure the rosary was this for my parents.

1

Many of the rituals of my early childhood seemed to vanish in the wake of the Second Vatican Council. In the attempt to make prayer more personal and more comprehensible for all of us, the Council modified many traditions and prayers that had lost their religious meaning or that tended to obscure the central issues of faith. The spirituality that blossomed as a result focused on scriptural and contemplative prayer, bringing a breath of new life to the church. Many of the memorized formulas, however, and prescribed conventions of an earlier age disappeared in the process. The loss of these rituals and rote prayers has left many Catholics who grew up after the Council feeling bereft, deprived of an identity that my generation took for granted, and searching for a way to share prayer with their children.

This book is an attempt to give families a guide for prayer and ritual. Part One offers simple rote prayers for both traditional times of prayer as well as those less traditional times when we might feel moved to pray. Some prayers suggest simple ritual actions to emphasize the meaning of the prayer and to involve children more fully. Also included are prayers from tradition that many of us have forgotten or were never taught, and prayers for different occasions from the Psalms. Several prayers are offered for each situation, so that parents can choose the ones most comfortable for them and for their children.

The focus in this first section is on developing personal prayer, making prayer the natural response of the individual to everything from waking to sleeping, from housework to study, from leaving to returning home. The hope is that certain activities of both parents and children will become so strongly associated with prayer that prayer becomes the automatic response to the action. While some of these prayers in this section are meant to be shared, such as meal blessings, the primary intent here is for each of us to learn to pray throughout our day.

The rituals in Part Two are focused on family prayer. They offer simple ways for a family to "prayerfully" celebrate special family events such as losing the first tooth, learning to ride a bike, having a new baby, and moving to a new home. These rituals encourage family members to support one another, to applaud each other's successes, and to mourn for each other's losses. They offer a sense of family identity, of belonging to a community where the events in the life of each individual are important and sacred, and the life of the family as a whole is worth our attention and celebration.

Part Three offers ideas for ritualizing the important holidays and holy days of the year. These rituals offer families a way to foster a sense of Christian identity. What does it mean for our family to belong to the larger, Catholic Christian community? How can we celebrate special feasts and hand on traditions that will help our children understand who they are in our multicultural world? How can we ritualize what we believe in such a way that our children develop confidence in their own identity, and do not feel threatened by another's truth? Many of these rituals involve simple family activities designed to make prayer time more appealing.

Finally, in Part Four, you will find a new look at some ancient Catholic traditions, such as litanies and novenas. This section reminds us of our Catholic roots, while providing some contemporary insights. These prayers can be used for either personal or family prayer.

HOW TO START

If you have never tried prayer in your family, begin with a simple bedtime and morning prayer. Remember, even if you feel uncomfortable with this, a young child will view a simple prayer ritual in the same natural way that he or she accepts any new game or activity. The sign of the cross is not far from "Itsy, Bitsy Spider" in the mind of the two-year-old.

The rote learning of prayers precedes understanding, but if the learning is there, understanding has an opportunity to follow. The strength of memorized prayer is that these prayers become like a default setting on the computer; when we feel desperately in need of prayer but totally unable to pray, the simple, memorized formulas take over, offering us words for what we cannot express.

When you have become comfortable praying in the morning or evening, or both, the next simplest time to pray is at meals. Choose a meal prayer that fits your needs as well as the ages of your children, and pray it regularly. For your first attempt at family ritual, a holiday celebration like Thanksgiving or Christmas can be a good starting point. Rituals that involve making something, such as an Advent wreath or Jesse tree, are often more comfortable for parents unaccustomed to prayer. Significant events, like moving to a new home or the birth of a baby, can also provide an opening for ritual prayer.

No one family will want to use all the rituals or learn all the prayers given here. A large number have been included simply to offer you choices, not to make you feel guilty. All of the rituals can be adapted to fit your own family style and needs, and require some preparation. While it is not important who does the preparation, it is very important not to let the responsibility for prayer rest on one person alone, particularly not on one parent in a dual parent family.

One of the most important aspects of ritual is repetition. Consider carefully which holidays, events, and special times your family will want to continue celebrating. Choose these, modify the rituals as needed, then make them part of your family heritage. Making rituals a regular part of your family life will offer both you and your children a sense of security and predictability in an insecure, unpredictable world.

Scripture instructs us to pray unceasingly, to let all our being bless the Lord. It is my hope that this guide will become a source of support for all our families as we learn to pray always, all ways.

THE SIGN OF THE CROSS

In the name of the Father,

and of the Son,

and of the Holy Spirit. Amen.

PART I

PRAYER

THROUGHOUT

THE DAY

MORNING PRAYER

Personal prayer is the ongoing conversation between the individual and God, an awareness of the presence of God that permeates all of life. Living in the presence of God means making prayer the natural response to everything we do, from waking to sleeping, from housework to study, from leaving to returning home.

Just as the longest journey begins with taking the first step, making the whole day a prayer begins with the first moment. Rote prayers, those prayers we learn "by heart," provide an easy, comfortable way for us to pray at any time, but especially in the morning. The words are there for us before we are awake enough to think, or when we are too troubled, too frustrated, or just too rushed to be able to think. Simple gestures added to the words bring our whole bodies into our prayer and provide valuable memory aids for young children.

Choose a simple morning prayer to say with your child when you pick him up from the crib or wake her up for school. By the time your child is capable of remembering the words, the prayer will have become second nature. It will be known "by heart." If you choose a prayer with motions, such as making a cross on the eyes, do the actions for your young children as you say the words. Encourage your older children to pray when they awaken, or say a brief prayer with them on your first encounter of the day.

Fostering a sense of personal prayer in our children begins with becoming people of prayer ourselves. Choose a psalm or reflection for your own morning prayer. Recite it faithfully until it is committed to memory and can be triggered each morning by the baby's cry, the first light, or the alarm clock.

Prayer to be said on first opening your eyes...

> Let your gift of light fill this day, Lord,
> that we may be salt for the earth
> and light for the world.

9

PRAYERS ON AWAKENING

This prayer is appropriate throughout the child's growing years.

Lord,
open my eyes to see beauty (make a cross on each eye),
open my ears to hear truth (make a cross on each ear),
open my mouth to speak kindness (make a cross on the lips),
open my mind to seek wisdom (make a cross on the forehead),
open my heart to love (make a cross over the heart). Amen.

Keep me, God, as the apple of your eye;
hide me in the shadow of your wings
from all that would hurt me. (Psalm 17:8)

For all ages...say while making the sign of the cross.

Blessed be God who gives us a new day
and the chance to begin again. Amen.

From the rising of the sun (hands uplifted)
to its setting (bring hands down into folded position),
let the name of the Lord be praised (make the sign of the cross).

The total body motion in this prayer is helpful to a young child. Begin with your head bowed and eyes closed, turn toward a window, open your eyes, and raise your head.

As the earth turns to the sun,
teach us to turn to you, Lord. Amen.

This can be a comforting psalm for the preteen and teen years.

At dawn, let me hear of your steadfast love,
for in you I put my trust.
Teach me the way I should go,
for to you I lift up my soul.
Save me, Lord, from all that would hurt me,
for you are my God. (Psalm 143:8–9)

MORNING OFFERINGS

For the young child…

Lord, today, I offer you
all I think and say and do.
When I work and when I play,
be with me all through the day.

This simple phrase can be taught early, and grow with a child.

Thank you, Lord, for another day.
Let everything I do and say
be for your honor and glory.

A psalm prayer to use before asking God for needs of the day…

O Lord,
in the morning, you hear my voice,
in the morning, I bring my prayer before you,
and wait for you to answer. (Psalm 5:3)

The traditional morning offering...

O Jesus, through the Immaculate Heart of Mary, I offer you my prayers, works, joys, and sufferings of this day, in union with the holy sacrifice of the Mass throughout the world. I offer them for all the intentions of your Sacred Heart: the salvation of souls, reparation for sin, and the reunion of all Christians. I offer them for the intentions of our bishops and of all members of the apostleship of prayer, and in particular, for those recommended by our Holy Father this month. Amen.

Give thanks to the Lord who is good.
God's steadfast love endures forever.
(Psalm 118:1)

A comforting psalm prayer for parents and older children...

The law of the Lord is perfect
   new life for the soul;
The decree of the Lord is trustworthy,
   wisdom for the simple.
The precepts of the Lord are right,
   joy for the heart.
The command of the Lord is clear,
   light for the eyes. (Psalm 19:7–8)

A beautiful morning psalm to say with a child...

I will bless the Lord at all times;
God's praise shall be ever in my mouth.
Let my soul glory in the Lord;
let the humble hear and be glad.
Come! Glorify the Lord with me,
together let us praise God's name.
(Psalm 34:1–4)

A prayer for repeating throughout the day...
Remain with me the whole day, Lord.
Let your grace be a sun that never sets.

Day by day we bless you, Lord.
We praise your name forever.

GUARDIAN ANGEL PRAYERS

Angels have recently come into the limelight and gained acceptance in general society. As a church, we have always believed in angels, particularly the angel given the task of caring for us, our guardian angel. Encourage a prayer to the guardian angel at the start of each day.

From tradition...

Angel of God, my guardian dear,
to whom God's love commits me here;
Ever this day be at my side,
to light and guard, to rule and guide. Amen.

Another version for the very young child...

Guardian angel, protect me today,
watch over me while I work and play.
Let me be kind and loving and good,
help me to do the things I should.

13

FOR PARENTS

A prayer to be said on awakening...

Lord,
    you have given me this day.
Thank you for the seconds, the minutes, the hours,
    measured by the earth's journey
    as it spins recklessly on its way.
I cannot control the day,
    any more than I can control the earth,
    whose motion shapes the hours.
Help me not to grasp greedily at the minutes,
    filling the hours with too many efforts.
Keep me attentive
    to you
    to others,
    to the earth itself...
As the time
    slips gently through my fingers.
Let my actions begin in peace
    and become a song of praise. Amen.

A prayer to be said before picking a child up from the crib...

Lord,
help me to hear you calling
in the voice of my child.
Let me see you in the eyes that look into mine,
feel your embrace in the arms that close around me,
and know that I am loved,
even as I teach my child
what it means to be loved. Amen.

Here is a blessing to be given to a child when you wake her, or at the first morning greeting.

Lord,

Bless N..., and fill her day with your peace (make a cross on the child's forehead).

Help us to meet this day's responsibilities.

Let nothing separate us from your love. Amen.

A parent's morning prayer...

Lord, teach me goodness, discipline, and wisdom,
and help me to teach them to my children.
Let these gifts keep us from becoming hardened by evil,
weakened by laziness,
or ignorant because of foolishness. Amen.

This is one of the most comforting of the psalms, especially in times of trouble.

You, Lord, are my shepherd;
    I shall not want.
In green meadows, you give me repose;
    Beside restful waters you lead me; you refresh my soul.
You guide me in right paths for your name's sake.
Even though I walk through the darkest valley, I fear no evil:
    For you are at my side;
    With your rod and your staff you comfort me.
You prepare a feast for me in the presence of my enemies;
    You anoint my head with oil; my cup overflows.
Surely goodness and kindness will follow me all the days of my life;
    And I shall dwell in the house of the Lord
    my whole life long. (Psalm 23)

THE LORD'S PRAYER

Our Father, who art in heaven, hallowed be your name, your kingdom come, your will be done, on earth as it is in heaven. Give us this day our daily bread and forgive us our trespasses, as we forgive those who trespass against us. And lead us not into temptation, but deliver us from evil. Amen.

A prayer of praise...

Your steadfast love, O Lord,
　reaches to the heavens;
　your faithfulness to the clouds.
Your justice is like the mighty mountains,
　your judgments are like the deep sea...
　all people may take refuge in your wings. (Psalm 36:5–7)

A psalm prayer of rejoicing for the beautiful mornings and evenings.
The heavens are telling the glory of God
and the stars are proclaiming God's handiwork.
Each day teaches the new day
and each night hands on this knowledge. (Psalm 19:1–2)

This traditional morning prayer to Mary can also be used in time of need.

MEMORARE

Remember, O most gracious Virgin Mary, that never was it known that anyone who fled to your protection, implored your help, or sought your intercession was left unaided. Inspired by this confidence, I fly unto you, O Virgin of virgins, my Mother. To you I come, before you I stand, sinful and sorrowful. O Mother of the Word Incarnate, do not despise my petitions, but in your mercy hear and answer me. Amen.

BREASTPLATE OF ST. PATRICK

Here is a prayer for difficult times, based on the traditional prayer known as the "Breastplate of St. Patrick."

This Day God Gives Me

This day God gives me strength of high heaven,
    Sun and moon shining, flame in my hearth,
Flashing of lightning, wind in its swiftness,
    Deeps of the ocean, firmness of earth.

This day God sends me strength as my guardian,
    Might to uphold me, wisdom as guide,
Your eyes are watchful, your ears are listening,
    Your lips are speaking, friend at my side.

God's way is my way, God's shield is round me
    God's host defends me, saving from ill.
Angels of heaven, drive from me always
    All that would harm me, stand by me still.

Rising, I thank you, mighty and strong One,
    King of creation, Giver of rest,
Firmly confessing threeness of Persons,
    Oneness of Godhead, Trinity blest.

(Text attributed to St. Patrick, adapted by James Quinn, SJ, © 1969.
Used by permission of Selah Publishing Co., Inc., Kingston, NY 12401. All rights reserved.)

Another translation of the St. Patrick prayer...

I arise today
    through God's strength to pilot me
    God's might to uphold me
    God's wisdom to guide me
    God's eye to look before me
    God's ear to hear me
    God's way to lie before me
    God's shield to protect me
    God's angels to save me from harm.

EVENING PRAYER

Bedtime has become the usual time in families for sharing prayer with children. The end of the day, with its rituals of going to sleep and letting go of con-

sciousness and light, can be frightening for children. Evening prayer is a comforting ritual that reassures children that God will be watching over them. In our family, it was a time for individual attention and quiet intimacy with each of our children.

Most of us remember a "God bless..." list from our childhood, usually prayed after one or two traditional, memorized prayers. You'll find those traditional prayers in this book, either here or in Morning Prayer. The other prayers and psalms offered here are not meant to replace "God bless Mommy, etc." Instead, they are meant to provide simple phrases that can grow with your children, brief prayers to say even on those nights when they are too tired to pray. Choose one or two that you and your child will both enjoy.

This time of quiet at the end of the day is a good time to begin teaching spontaneous prayer, that is, using your own thoughts and words to form a prayer. When the usual prayer you have chosen for bed has been said, invite your children to thank God for the beautiful things they saw and did during the day and to ask for any special needs that they, or their family or friends, may have.

Bedtime is also a good time for considering our failings during the day. Check the section on forgiveness for ways to end the day with a simple recognition of our failings, with prayers and gestures of reconciliation.

Say while making the sign of the cross.

Bless me, Lord, as this day ends,
   bless my family and my friends.
Keep me safe all through the night,
   wake me with the morning's light. Amen.
God bless (N...).

A comforting psalm prayer...

I lie down to sleep,
     knowing I will wake again,
     for God takes care of me. (Psalm 3:6)

HAIL MARY

Hail Mary, full of grace, the Lord is with you. Blessed are you among women and blessed is the fruit of your womb, Jesus. Holy Mary, Mother of God, pray for us sinners, now and at the hour of our death. Amen.

ANGEL PRAYERS

Here is a guardian angel prayer that can be said at bedtime.

Angel of God, my guardian dear,
     to whom God's love commits me here;
Watch over me throughout the night,
     keep me safe within your sight.

Hebrew tradition recognizes four angels with various tasks in guiding our lives, all with responsibility for protecting the child.

Four angels gathered 'round my bed,
Ariel, angel of light, at my head,
Gabriel, messenger, at my feet,
watch over me now as I sleep.
Michael, defender, on my right,
keep me safe all through the night.
Raphael, healer, at my left stay,
bring me strength for a brand new day.
Four angels watching, bending near,
protect me now from harm and fear.

PRAYER OF ST. FRANCIS

Lord, make me an instrument of your peace.
Where there is hatred, let me sow love;
    where there is injury, pardon;
    where there is doubt, faith;
    where there is despair, hope;
    where there is darkness, light;
    and where there is sadness, joy.
O divine Master, grant that I may not so much seek
    to be consoled, as to console,
    to be understood, as to understand,
    to be loved, as to love.
For it is in giving that we receive;
    in pardoning that we are pardoned;
    and in dying that we are born to eternal life.

Into your hands, Lord,
I commit my spirit. (Psalm 31:5)

GLORY BE

Glory be to the Father, and to the Son, and to the Holy Spirit,
as it was in the beginning is now, and ever shall be, world without end. Amen.

BLESSINGS FOR THE END OF THE DAY

The sacrament of Baptism reminds us of the right and duty of parents to bless their children. Bedtime is a wonderful time to develop the habit of laying your hands gently on a child's head and pronouncing a simple blessing. The following blessings are paraphrased from Scripture and from the Night Prayer of the church.

Say while tracing a cross on the child's forehead...

May the Lord bless you with peace,
  close your eyes in restful sleep,
  and wake you with joy in the morning.

Lay both hands on child's head...

May the Lord protect and defend you
  and keep you from all harm.

May the Lord protect you when you are awake (make a cross on
child's forehead),
  watch over you when you sleep (make a cross on child's eyes),
  that awake, you may keep watch with Christ,
  and asleep, rest in his peace (making cross on child's heart).

Trace a cross on a child's forehead...

Lie down in peace
let sleep come at once.
For the Lord watches over you
and keeps you safe. (Psalm 4:8)

PARENT MEDITATIONS
A prayer for the end of a bad day...

Lord,
Into your hands, I entrust my child.
We have had a bad day
  she was so difficult
  so whiny;
I overreacted.

21

I shouted "grow up"...
I forgot that's what she's trying to do,
   that's why she needs me.
Forgive me for the times I failed today,
   failed to be patient,
   failed to be understanding and kind,
   failed to be consistent and firm,
   failed to listen.
Help my child to forgive me.
Help me to remember
   a bad day is not a bad life,
   that you have made the perfect gift for imperfect parents...
Tomorrow.
Amen.

After a good day...

Into your hands, Lord, I entrust my child.
Today was one of those perfect days
when I know I am doing it right
and it feels good to be a parent.
Today, I was able to kiss the hurt away.
Today I had the answers to the questions,
and the time to share the wonder.
Today I saw you shining in the eyes of my child,
today, I think he found you in mine.
Thank you for a good day.
Help me to remember
that a good day is not a good life,
that you have made the perfect gift for perfect parents...
Tomorrow.
Amen.

For parent insomniacs…

O Lord, let your face shine on us!
Put gladness into our hearts,
　　so that as soon as we lie down,
　　we fall peacefully asleep,
　　knowing that you alone, Lord,
　　bring security to our home. (Psalm 4:6–8)

A psalm for the close of a good day…

I will give thanks to the Lord with all my heart;
I will tell of all your wonderful deeds.
I will be glad and exult in you;
I will sing praise to your name, most high.
(Psalm 9:1–2)

PRAYERS FOR PROTECTION

Protect us, Lord, when we stay awake,
　　watch over us when we sleep.
Awake, let us keep watch with Christ;
　　asleep, let us rest in his peace. Amen.

Sister Una O'Connor, C.P., provided this prayer, known as the Dedication of the Home to Mary. It is a beautiful prayer for protection on ending the day.

Holy Mary, Mother of God, we choose you today as the lady and mistress of this house. Preserve it from fire and water; from lightning and storms; from disease and hunger; from violence and untruth; from earthquakes and from sudden death. Bless and protect all who live here. Save them from every accident and misfortune, and keep them from evil.

MEAL BLESSINGS

One of the most sacred things we can do as parents is to gather the family for a meal. Food is not the issue here; we can gather just as well around frozen dinners or peanut butter and jelly as we can over lobster or steak. The issue is finding time to be family, to acknowledge our need for one another, and to learn to discuss and to share with people who care about us.

My father always worked well beyond our dinner hour. When he would come home, usually close to our bedtimes, we would sit down around our kitchen table for a cup of weak tea while he ate his supper and asked us about our day. Sometimes, we simply listened while he and my mother discussed an issue of importance to the family. Looking back, I am amazed at my mother's creativity in creating a family meal where none seemed possible.

For some people, the family meal may be breakfast, or lunch, or a different meal on different days, but a family that hopes to develop strong family ties must make an effort to share a meal several times a week. Family is the first place where we experience community. If children are ever to understand church as a praying community, they must first learn to celebrate simple ritual prayer within the family. A ritual uses symbolic actions and words to express a spiritual reality.

Once you have adopted a meal time, decide on the form of prayer you will use. A lighted candle can be added for Sundays and special meals. While there are many more involved meal blessings included in this text under the rituals for special family times and special times of the year, it is important to develop an "ordinary" ritual for the "ordinary" time in the life of the family. It is equally important to use a format that is repeated daily, so that everyone grows comfortable with the ritual.

Develop a traditional attitude for prayer. For some families, that may mean beginning with a sign of the cross and folding hands. Our family always holds hands around the table as a symbol of our unity. We have also traditionally allowed a short moment of silence when we first join hands, simply to give everyone the opportunity to get into a prayerful mind-set. (Sometimes a moment is needed just to get everyone to stop talking.)

24

Grace before meals has always been spontaneous in our house, but with the same basic format. First, we ask God's blessing on the food and ask God's blessing on the people gathered around the table, in particular, any guests and their families. We then thank God for the blessings of the day (each person thanking God for something), ask God for any special needs, and ask God to keep us mindful of those who have less.

GRACE BEFORE MEALS
A typical grace in our house might sound like this...
Bless us, Lord, and bless this food.
Bless especially our guest, N..., and her family.
Thank you for....
Please be with... (or pray for a particular need).
Keep us always mindful of those who have less. Amen.

Grace can also take the form of a simple litany of praise with responses.

Leader: Lord, you nourish us with bread from the earth,
Response: Blessed be God forever.
Leader: Lord, you refresh us with water from the rock,
and fruit from the vine,
Response: Blessed be God forever.
Leader: Lord, you provide for all our needs,
Response: Blessed be God forever.

Traditional Catholic grace...
Bless us, O Lord, and these your gifts, which we are about to receive from your bounty. Through Christ, our Lord. Amen.

Grace from the Jewish tradition...
Lift up your hands toward the sanctuary and bless the Lord.
Blessed are You, O Lord our God, King of the universe,
who brings forth bread from the earth. Amen.

25

Grace from the Protestant tradition...

Bless, O Lord, this food to our use, and us to your service, and make us ever mindful of the needs of others, in Jesus' name. Amen.

SPECIAL GRACE FOR SUNDAYS

Have your child light a candle while saying this prayer...

Parent: You came to bring light to our darkness;
Response: Help us to become a light to the world.

Your traditional grace follows. At the end of the meal, one child extinguishes the candle, and says...

Child: Carry the light within you.

GRACE AFTER MEALS

We have always found it more difficult to pray as a family after meals. Begin with grace before meals, and when your family has become comfortable with that, you can introduce grace after meals.

We thank you, Lord, for providing for your children. Keep us ever mindful of the needs of others less fortunate than ourselves. Amen.

Leader: Give thanks to the Lord, who is good.
Response: God's love is everlasting. (Psalm 106:1)

This is a traditional form of grace after meals...

We give you thanks, Almighty God, for all the benefits which we have received from your goodness. Through Christ, our Lord. Amen.

PRAYER FOR ORDINARY TIMES

Our role, as parents, is to teach our children to ask God's blessing on all the actions of the day. Once your children have grown into the habit of morning and evening prayer, it is only a small step to invite them to pray at other times.

Begin by saying prayers for them or with them. The younger they are when you begin, the more comfortable they will be with the tradition of blessing God for all things and at all times. If your children are older when you first attempt to introduce prayer, ask them at which times they would like to say a special prayer. The prayers given here are simply to help you to get started. As you become more comfortable and confident, make up your own prayers for all the actions of the day, and invite your children to do the same.

MAKING BEDS

Let the rest we have enjoyed, Lord,
    bring peace and order to our day.

PREPARING LUNCHES

Bless these lunches, Lord,
    and let this food nourish my children's bodies
    as my love for them nourishes their spirits.

FOR THE SCHOOL BUS DRIVER

Bless the bus driver, Lord,
    and protect the children we trust to his (her) care.
Send your angels to bear them up
    and deliver them safely. Amen.

27

FOR TEACHERS

Lord, bless this teacher (or N...) to whom we entrust our child.
Give her the patience to listen respectfully,
   the understanding to discipline gently,
   the diligence to explain carefully,
   the humor to laugh joyfully.
Bless her with the wisdom to see the giftedness in every child
   and the creativity and love to call it forth. Amen.

BLESSINGS ON LEAVING THE HOUSE

Leaving the house, like bedtime, is a time that lends itself to a blessing or prayer. Put something by the door, the way we once put holy water fonts, to remind everyone that comings and goings are sacred. A small cross will do, or a holy water font, if you have one. (When I was growing up, my mother kept an old Irish blessing next to our door.)

Choose a simple prayer or blessing that you and other family members feel comfortable saying. Make it a practice to say this prayer or blessing as you leave the house. Always let your children know they are loved before they leave the house, and gently remind them to do the same for you with words or a gesture such as a goodbye kiss. None of us ever has any assurance that we will always have another opportunity to express our love to our family.

For these blessings, place both hands on a child's head, or make a small cross on the forehead, or just give a warm hug.

May God bless you and bring you back safely.
Go in peace.

May the Lord bless you and keep you.
May the Lord's face shine upon you,
   and be gracious to you,
May God look upon you with kindness
and give you peace. (Numbers 6:24–26)

28

An old Irish blessing...

> May the road rise up to meet you;
> May the wind be always at your back;
> May the sun shine warm upon your face
>   and the rains fall soft upon your fields.
> And until we meet again,
>   may God hold you in the palm of his hand.

> God be with you
> and the angels keep watch over you.

ON ENTERING THE HOUSE

Take time as children enter to stop whatever you are doing and greet them with a hug and a simple prayer.

> Lord, help us to be present to you in one another. Amen.

> One thing I ask of the Lord...
> this I seek:
> To dwell in the house of the Lord
> all the days of my life. (Psalm 27:4)

PRAYERS BEFORE STUDY

A sign of the cross is made as this prayer is spoken...

> God of wisdom,
> May everything we do begin with your inspiration, (hand touches forehead),
>   continue with your help (hand touches chest),
>   and be completed (left shoulder),
>   in your love (right shoulder). Amen.

29

Here is a beautiful study prayer from the Psalms.
Your ways, O Lord, make known to me
(make a small cross on the forehead);
teach me your paths (make a small cross on the lips).
Lead me in your truth and teach me (make a small cross on the heart),
for you are the God of my salvation. (Psalm 25:4–5)

This is the traditional prayer before study.

Come, Holy Spirit, fill the hearts of your faithful,
and kindle in them the fire of your love.
Send forth your spirit
and they shall be created.
And you shall renew the face of the earth.

O God, you instructed the hearts of your faithful
by the light of the Holy Spirit.
Grant us in the same Holy Spirit, to be truly wise
and ever rejoice in his consolation.
Through Christ, our Lord. Amen.

These simple psalm prayers are wonderful ways to pray before a test:

Your ways, O Lord, make known to me;
teach me your paths. (Psalm 25:4)

Keep your kindness before my eyes;
I walk in your truth. (Psalm 26:3)

Show me, O Lord, your way,
and lead me on a level path. (Psalm 26:11)

BEFORE A SPORTING EVENT

Say this prayer with or for a child before a track meet, softball game, or other sporting event.

> Those who wait for the Lord
>   shall renew their strength,
> They shall mount up with wings like eagles,
>   they shall run and not be weary.
> They shall strive and not be faint. (Isaiah 40:31)

BEFORE A FAMILY TASK

> **Parents:**   Lord, let your light shine on us today.
> **Children:** Direct the work of our hands.

The prayer of St. Francis is especially appropriate before family tasks that serve the community. You will find this prayer on page 20, in the section on Evening Prayer. Pray it together before taking part in a community service activity, or work of social justice.

SETTING THE TABLE

> Lord God, bless this table and all who gather here.
> Help us to remember, Lord,
>   that you are the unseen guest at every meal.

WHEN GIVING ALLOWANCES

Weekly allowances are one of the ways we teach children responsibility. It is important that we teach, at the same time, the obligation we have to use our resources wisely and to care for the community. Giving allowances on a Sunday morning and asking the children to first set aside money for church and other "good deeds" teaches the concept of stewardship.

Parents can say this prayer while giving allowances to their children.

> Lord, all that we have is yours.
> Teach us to use your gifts wisely,
>   for ourselves and others.

THE APOSTLES' CREED

Sunday is a good time to remember what we believe as Christians. The Creed can be part of Sunday meal blessings, or morning or evening prayer.

> I believe in God, the Father almighty, creator of heaven and earth. I believe in Jesus Christ, his only son, our Lord, who was conceived by the Holy Spirit, born of the Virgin Mary, suffered under Pontius Pilate, was crucified, died, and was buried. He descended to the dead; on the third day he rose again. He ascended into heaven, and is seated at the right hand of the Father; he will come again to judge the living and the dead. I believe in the Holy Spirit, the holy catholic Church, the communion of saints, the forgiveness of sins, the resurrection of the body, and life everlasting. Amen.

IN TIMES OF ANGER

Instead of teaching children to count to ten before they speak when they are angry, teach them to close their lips and quietly say the following verse from the Psalms. It takes less than ten seconds, but is very effective. Use this prayer when you are angry, as well. This is also a helpful prayer when one is tempted to lie.

> Set a guard over my mouth, O Lord;
>   keep watch over the door of my lips. (Psalm 141:3)

In Times of Need

A psalm prayer to teach children to say when they are frightened.

Guard me as the apple of your eye;
  hide me in the shadow of your wings
  from all who would hurt me. (Psalm 17:8–9)

The following psalms are good choices for times of need:

To you, O Lord, I lift up my soul.
O my God, in you I trust;
  do not let me not be put to shame. (Psalm 25:1)

Answer me when I call, O God.
Be gracious to me, hear my prayer. (Psalm 4:1)

In you, O Lord, I take refuge,
  do not let me be put to shame.
In your justice deliver me,
  incline your ear to me,
Hurry and rescue me. (Psalm 31:1–2)

O Lord, do not be far from me.
Come quickly to help me. (Psalm 22:19)

The Memorare is a traditional prayer for help in times of need. When I was a child, we were taught that if you prayed the Memorare thirteen times in succession, Mary could not let you down. While the idea is somewhat superstitious, the repetition is comforting in times of fear and great need. You can find the Memorare on page 16, in the section on Morning Prayer.

One of the best ways to petition God for assistance is to say thank you in expectation of what God will do for us. These two New Testament passages model that type of expectant prayer.

Glory be to God,
    whose power working in us
    can accomplish infinitely more
    than we can ask or imagine. (Ephesians 3:20)

I am convinced that neither death nor life,
    nor angels nor rulers,
    nor things present nor things to come,
    nor powers, nor height, nor depth,
    nor anything else in all creation,
will be able to separate us from the love of God
    in Christ Jesus our Lord. (Romans 8:38–39)

PRAYER TO ST. MICHAEL THE ARCHANGEL
A traditional church prayer for confronting evil...

St. Michael, the archangel, defend us in battle. Be our safeguard against the wickedness and snares of the enemy. Rebuke him, O God, we humbly beseech thee, and do thou O Prince of the heavenly host, by thy divine power, cast into hell Satan and all the other evil spirits who wander through the world seeking the destruction of souls. Amen.

IN TIMES OF WAITING
Use this while waiting in line, in the grocery store, in traffic...

Lord, let nothing rob me of your peace.
Remind me gently of all those who have waited for me.

When waiting with a child under six, try this counting game. After doing the first three numbers, make up the rest; for example, "four" might be "for your birthday coming in June," "five for the family, we'll see them soon," until you get to ten.

One, for the God who waits for me.
Two, for the Son who came for me.
Three, for the Spirit who sets us free.
Four… (continue rhyme through nine).
Ten, for the minutes we waited in line,
The gift of waiting is sharing time.

While waiting for an answer to prayer…

Lord, God of all time and all waiting,
give us patience to await your time,
wisdom to use the time of waiting well,
and hope to trust in your answer. Amen.

Our soul waits for the Lord,
who is our help and our shield.
In God our hearts rejoice
because we trust in the Lord's holy name.
Let your steadfast love, O Lord,
be upon us, even as we hope in you. (Psalm 33:21–22)

IN TIMES OF JOY

The Psalms are filled with expressions of joy, and older children might enjoy learning a few of them. Teach younger children to say a simple "Thank you, God," for the good things in life.

Give thanks to the Lord who is good;
God's love is everlasting. (Psalm 136:1)

Bless the Lord, my soul,
let all my being bless God's holy name. (Psalm 103:1)

This is Mary's great song of joy.

THE MAGNIFICAT

My soul magnifies the Lord,
and my spirit rejoices in God my Savior,
for you have looked with favor on the lowliness of your servant.
Surely, from now on all generations will call me blessed;
for you, the almighty, have done great things for me,
and holy is your name.
Your mercy is for those who fear you
from generation to generation.
You have shown strength with your arm;
you have scattered the proud in the thoughts of their hearts.
You have brought down the powerful from their thrones,
and lifted up the lowly;
You have filled the hungry with good things,
and sent the rich away empty.
You have helped your servant Israel,
in remembrance of your mercy,
according to the promise you made to our ancestors,
to Abraham and to his descendants forever. (Luke 1:47–55)

FORGIVENESS PRAYERS

Forgiveness is one of the most important virtues any of us can learn. The inability to forgive has destroyed families, ripped societies apart, and stirred

up wars. Hatred and revenge can be all-consuming and all-absorbing, poisoning our entire lives. When Jesus taught us to love our enemies, I suspect it was more for our benefit than theirs; he knew that hatred would destroy us.

We learn forgiveness not just by being forgiven, but by being asked to forgive. Parents who are willing to acknowledge that they have been unjust, crabby, short-tempered, or mean, and who ask forgiveness of their children, will raise children who are better able to recognize their own shortcomings and more willing to ask forgiveness. Forgiveness offers children the freedom to make mistakes and fail, knowing that they will still be loved. Practicing forgiveness is a constant reminder to the child that our actions have a social dimension, and that it is our responsibility to consider the effect they will have on others.

Acknowledging our failings is the first step to overcoming them. Often, though, we are too angry and upset to ask forgiveness at the moment we have done something wrong. Setting aside time at the end of each day—at bedtime, at supper, or another moment in the evening—gives us all a chance to review the things we did well and the ones that could have been done better or differently.

If there has been any anger or unpleasantness in the family during the day, this is the time to bring some peace to the situation. This is also the time for parents and children to say they are sorry for any hurt they may have caused each other during the day. Once this has become an established habit, it will be easier for everyone in our families to understand the importance of asking forgiveness, and of ending the day with an act of sorrow for any wrongs that have been committed.

Let your steadfast love, O Lord, be upon us,
even as we hope in you. (Psalm 33:22)

37

FAMILY LITANY

The following litany is said with the parent saying the verse and response first, and the child repeating it. It can be said with children individually, or with the family as a whole.

Parent:	For the times I was impatient today, forgive me Lord.
Child:	For the times I was impatient today, forgive me, Lord.
Parent:	For the times I did not listen today, forgive me, Lord.
Child:	(Repeat parent petition...).
Parent:	For the times I was unkind today, forgive me, Lord.
Parent:	For the times I was selfish today, forgive me, Lord.
Parent:	For any time I was not honest today, forgive me, Lord.

At this moment, the parent(s) shares anything from the day for which she or he is particularly sorry, asking forgiveness of the child(ren). Each child is then invited to do the same. End with the Jesus Prayer given here, or with another act of sorrow or contrition, or with a line from one of the Psalms.

JESUS PRAYER

Lord, Jesus Christ, son of the living God,
 have mercy on me, a sinner.

May God be gracious to us and bless us,
may the face of the Lord shine upon us. (Psalm 67:1)

ACT OF CONTRITION

This is the traditional act of contrition.

O, my God! I am heartily sorry for having offended you. And I detest all my sins, because I dread the loss of heaven and the pains of hell. But most of all, because they offend you, my God, who are all good and deserving of all my love. I firmly resolve with the help of your grace, to confess my sins, to do penance, and to amend my life. Amen.

This newer version emphasizes the love of God over the fear of punishment.

O my God, I am sorry for sinning against you, because I love you with all my heart. I firmly intend, with your help, to make up for my sins, to sin no more, and to avoid whatever leads me to sin. Amen.

Be merciful to me, O God, be merciful to me,
for in you my soul takes refuge. (Psalm 57:1)

Psalm 51 is the great prayer of forgiveness in the church. The words are difficult for very young children, but either of the phrases given here might be helpful acts of contrition for adults and teens.

Have mercy on me, O God,
    according to your steadfast love;
According to your abundant mercy,
    blot out my transgressions.
Wash me from my guilt
    and cleanse me from my sin. (Psalm 51:1–2)

Create in me a clean heart, O God,
and put a new and right spirit within me.
Do not cast me away from your presence,
and do not take your holy spirit from me. (Psalm 51:10–11)

This prayer for forgiveness was once said at the conclusion of each decade of the rosary.

O my Jesus, forgive us our sins,
    save us from the fires of hell.
Lead all souls to heaven,
    especially those in most need of your mercy.

CONFITEOR

I confess to almighty God, and to you my brothers and sisters, that I have sinned through my own fault, in my thoughts and in my words, in what I have done and in what I have failed to do, and I ask Blessed Mary, ever Virgin, and all the angels and saints to pray for me to the Lord our God.

PART II

RITUALS

FOR FAMILY

TIMES

IN every family, there are certain times that deserve celebration. These can be the holy days of the church, civic holidays, or special events within family life. A family ritual is an ideal way to commemorate these times.

The rituals given in this section will help you to recognize and note some of these special moments that occur within families. Don't limit your celebrating, though, to the feasts given here. Name your own holy days and special times, invite your children to do the same, then ritualize and celebrate!

WELCOMING A NEW BABY

Nothing is quite so wonderful or quite so disruptive to the life of a family as the birth of a new baby. While this is a joyous event, it also involves an enormous restructuring of roles within the family and is an adjustment process for all. A ritual to welcome a baby into the home can help to address some of these issues.

Tell the other children in your family that you would like to ask God's blessing on the baby and on the rest of the family as it begins a new phase of life. Explain that having a new baby takes a lot of work on everyone's part, and ask how they would like to help with these changes. Ask them about their fears, concerns, and expectations about having a new child in the house. Go through the ritual, demonstrating what you will do, so that it will be comfortable for everyone involved.

If you are just coming home from the hospital when you use this ritual, let the other children enter the house first, followed by the baby. This will give them the sense of leading the new member into their home. Next, gather in the living room or another comfortable place. Have a small dish of warm water nearby to use for blessing the baby.

One of the parents dips his or her thumb in the water and traces a cross on the baby's head, saying...

Parent: N...(baby's name), I bless you and welcome you to our family. I will try to ...(here mention a few things that

you will try to do for the baby), and I promise I will
always love you.

If two parents are present, have the other parent repeat this action. Then have each of the children do the same. If the children are too small, one of the parents can help them to make a sign of the cross and say the words for them. When all the children have blessed the baby, anyone else who is present is invited to bless the baby.

Parent: N..., we ask God to bless you throughout all your life. We ask God to bless us, as well, and help us be the family you will need.

All: Amen.

Welcoming the baby into your home is the beginning of this child's life of faith. Continue to nurture her faith journey by starting each day with a prayer, and ending each day with a blessing. Invite the other family members to pray regularly with the baby.

For Parents

Read this prayer often during the first few weeks with your new baby, and repeat it throughout her childhood.

Lord, you have chosen us
    to bring new life into the world.
Just as you made this child in your image and likeness,
    she will recreate you in our image.
Let the God we mirror for her
    be loving, forgiving, tender, and kind,
    ever present, ever watchful, ever gentle.
And may we come to know you in a new way
    through this new life you have entrusted to our care.

BIRTHDAYS

Birthdays are a typical family celebration. They allow families to focus on just one child at a time (usually) and to point out to the rest of the family how special that person is. Decorate for the birthday, and involve the other family members in planning and putting up the decorations. Make a special breakfast or a special dinner, birthday child's choice. Develop a traditional blessing for the birthday child, to be said each year on the birthday morning.

Place your hands on the child's head, or make a sign of the cross on his or her forehead, saying...

N..., may God bless you and fill your life with the same love and joy that your presence has brought to our home.

Or,

N..., for ...(age) years you have filled our home with joy. May God bless you as well with the peace and joy that you have brought to us.

Or,

God our Creator, maker of the universe, you have given us N... to fill our hearts with love and our home with joy. Bless him with many years to do your work and sing your praise.

Plan to hold a birthday ritual after the family meal. Even if a party is to be held on a separate day when young guests can attend, keep the ritual on the actual birth day. This is a sacred day in your family. Activities such as measuring the child and writing the height on the wall, taking a traditional picture (by a young tree, for example), can all be part of this ritual action.

In my husband's family, there was an evergreen tree in front of their house that appears in every important family picture, growing as the children grew. These traditions offer a sense of identity to the growing child.

45

A Birthday Ritual

Leader: The blessing of the Lord endures forever.

All: God's faithfulness is from age to age.

Leader: Lord God, we thank you for the life of N.... We especially want to thank you for his.... (Here, have each family member mention a special talent or gift of the birthday person. After each gift is mentioned, pray "We thank you, Lord.")

Leader: Lord, bless N... on this ... (age) birthday. Keep us all united as a family and give us many years together to love one another.

End this ritual with candles and cake. If you are not having the cake at this time, close with a simple song of love and appreciation, saving "Happy Birthday" for the cake and candles.

FIRST DAY OF SCHOOL

Starting kindergarten can be a stress-filled occasion for the young child. Invite each member of the family to prepare a little note or picture for the child who is beginning school, asking God's blessing for this special day. Preschoolers will need help in writing a prayer for their sibling; they can draw or use stickers for their note. The notes can be included as a surprise when you pack the child's lunch or snack for school.

This is an important day to bless your child before leaving, but keep it simple. For example, saying "God bless you and keep you, and give you a wonderful day" is more than enough. Don't pray for the year ahead. The young child has enough to do wondering about the next hour without bringing in another whole year. And the notes that you put in your child's lunchbox will be a gentle reminder of the family's love and support.

The first day of school is a new beginning for all school-age children, whether they are six or sixteen. Plan a special breakfast and begin with one of these prayers...

God of Wisdom,
May everything we do begin with your inspiration
(hand touches forehead),
    continue with your help (hand touches chest),
    and be completed (left shoulder),
    in your love (right shoulder). Amen.

Or,

Your ways, O Lord, make known to me
(make a small cross on the forehead);
    teach me your paths (make a small cross on the lips).
Guide me in your truth (make a small cross on the heart),
    for you are my God, my Savior.

Bless the children as you hand them their snacks or lunchboxes, placing a hand on their heads and tracing a small cross, saying:

May God bless you and keep you.
May the Lord's face shine upon you.
May God give you peace.

Or,

May God give the angels watch over you to keep you from harm. I bless you in the name of the God who creates, the God who redeems, and the God who makes us all holy. Amen.

Or,

God our creator, maker of the universe,
    you offer us learning to enrich our minds.
Bless N...'s search for knowledge
    and let all her learning become a prayer.

A note in the lunchbox is always appreciated, even by high schoolers, and can be a blessing in disguise.

For Parents
On the first day of school...

She looks so brave and independent, Lord,
    as she walks away from me.
I do not feel her courage; I feel alone.
I have done my best
    and now another will judge her,
    another will make demands of her.
She will be measured against her peers, not against my love.
Help her to find the wisdom to know her own self-worth,
    help her to find the simplicity to obey
    and the patience to wait quietly,
    help her to find her milk money, taped inside her lunchbox,
    help her to find the bathroom.
And Lord,
    help her to know she can always come home. Amen.

LEARNING TO RIDE A BIKE

There are certain moments in the lives of children that have great significance. While a baby learning to walk is a great event for parents, it is an inner-directed compulsion rather than a choice. Learning to ride a two-wheeler is a choice often accompanied by risk and the need to overcome fear. This is an occasion that deserves a special celebration.

Plan a little party after dinner for the child involved. Perhaps you can make or buy a cake decorated with a small keepsake, such as a plastic bicycle or little plastic cartoon figure, and the words "Congratulations" written on top. Take a moment to sit quietly after dinner, before dessert, while everyone is gathered at the table. Then begin this ritual:

Leader: This is the day that the Lord has made.
All: Let us rejoice and be glad in it.

48

Leader: Lord, today we celebrate the accomplishment of N...
who has just learned to ride a bike. You promised you
would raise us up on eagle's wings. We ask you to hold
him in your hands and protect him from harm. We thank
you, Lord, for all the gifts you give us that help us to get
from one place to another.

Leader: For cars...

All: We thank you, Lord.

Now invite family members to thank God for all the ways that help us to get around, such as buses, trains, planes, horses, trucks. All respond "We thank you, Lord" after each item is named. End ritual as follows:

Leader: For bicycles and for N...

All: We thank you, Lord. Amen.

A Prayer for Parents

Lord,
we removed the training wheels today
and he rode
confident and secure,
away from us,
as we cheered.
Help us to do our job as well as those small wheels,
parents—
training wheels for childhood—
providing balance
for the delicate process of growing.
Then, Lord,
help us to celebrate
help us not to resent
when we are no longer needed,
and he can ride on his own.

LOSING THE FIRST TOOTH

An event that always has great significance in the life of a child is losing the first tooth. It can be traumatic to lose a part of your body, and we parents attempt to ease the trauma with tooth fairies. It is also a very visible event, as most six-year-olds will be quick to demonstrate. A simple prayer service to celebrate losing a tooth can help the child see this moment as a sign that he or she is growing up.

Plan to celebrate with a prayer at the family meal and serve ice cream as a special, healing treat. Present the child with a new toothbrush. (Don't make too much of this; you don't want to have children pulling teeth out ahead of time!)

Parent: Let us bless the Lord.

All: Now and forever.

Parent: Lord, we thank you for N.... As a baby, he has given great joy to our family. We thank you for all the joy he will continue to give throughout his childhood. Help us to be a loving family and to support each other in all our growing.

All: Amen.

A VISIT FROM OUT-OF-TOWN RELATIVES OR FRIENDS

Some families grow up within traveling distance of all the relatives, knowing their cousins, aunts, and uncles from birth. But many children do not even meet some of their relatives until they are well into their childhood or teen years.

In my own family, all of my father's relatives still live in Ireland, and we met them for the first time when our youngest child was nine. We stepped out of customs in Shannon airport into a waiting area that held seven carloads of the O'Connell clan. (Other people traveling on the plane with us thought we must have been celebrities to have merited this welcome.) We felt incredibly welcomed and loved, and became very aware of the need for simple ways to break the ice with family members we had never met.

Start to plan at least a week prior to the visit for a special meal or picnic.

Invite everyone in the family to choose a few pictures, and one story about themselves that they would like to share with your guests. Ask the visitors to bring pictures and stories, too.

Keep the meal simple; the event will bring its own share of stress without adding to it. Begin the meal with a simple prayer of thanksgiving, such as this:

> **All:** Lord, we thank you for bringing us all together as family. Bless this food and bless our time together. We ask this in the name of Jesus. Amen.

Between the dinner and the dessert, ask everyone to share their stories. Children may want to share souvenirs or trophies instead of pictures. Be sure to let each person tell his or her own story, even if someone else remembers it differently.

By the time you are ready for dessert, your guests will have had a chance to learn something special about each one of you, and hopefully, they will have shared something special about themselves.

TAKING RISKS

When I asked my adult children what events should be ritualized in the life of a growing family, my older daughter, Becky, suggested moments of risk: trying out for a team, a chorus, or a play; standing up to your peers on an issue; starting a job; or taking an unpopular stand in a class that deals with social issues.

Risk taking is one of the most difficult acts an individual makes and the one most in need of support, especially during teen years. This ritual, based on Isaiah 43:1–3, can be adapted and changed for any event that causes worry and fear, from tryouts to exams. Celebrate it with the whole family after supper, or with the individual child before bed or before leaving for the event in question.

> **Leader:** Let us bless the Lord,
> **Response:** Now and forever.
> **Leader:** The Lord says, "Do not be afraid, for I have redeemed you. I have called you by name and you are mine."

Response: Be not afraid.

Leader: Should you pass through the sea, you will not drown.

Response: Be not afraid.

Leader: Should you walk through rivers, they will not swallow you.

Response: Be not afraid.

Leader: Should you walk through fire, you will not be scorched.

Response: Be not afraid.

Leader: For you are precious in my eyes, and honored, and I love you. God of courage, help us to remember that Peter would never have known he could walk on water if he had not gotten out of the boat. Help us to risk, to try our best, and never to let fear of failure keep us from reaching for our dreams.

Response: Amen.

For Parents

Parents need to pray for reassurance about their children, as well.

Lord, be with my child.
Enable him to do his best
    to be ready to accept failure or success.
Help me to be accepting, also.
Keep me from ever exerting pressure on my child
    to fulfill my dreams. Amen.

CELEBRATION OF FAILURE

We all learn much more from our failures than we do from our successes, if we are willing to stop and examine them. Children need to know that it's okay to fail, that people who never make mistakes never make much of anything. Most failures do not require special attention, and can be handled with the reassurance that the child can try again, coupled with an offer to help and a reminder of our love.

52

But some failures hurt more than others, and prayer can help ease the hurt. Healing prayer is needed any time someone in the family suffers a setback, such as not making the team, not getting the part in the play, studying hard for an exam but getting a "D," or losing in any significant fashion. This is probably not the time for a full ritual, just a simple, healing, family prayer. Use this prayer before your mealtime grace, or before going to bed.

Leader:	Let us bless the Lord,
All:	Now and forever.
Leader:	Lord, help us to remember that we can't always succeed, and that your love for us does not depend upon success. Help us to remember that good can come out of evil. Help us to let go of our pain.
All:	Heal us, O Lord.
Leader:	We pray too, Lord, for others who are hurting tonight. (Invite children to name others who may be suffering from some hurt.)
Response:	Heal us, O Lord.
All:	Glory be to the Father, and to the Son, and to the Holy Spirit. Amen.

CELEBRATION OF SUCCESS

Success is different for different people. Try to be open to the things your children consider real successes in their lives. Let them tell you when they would like to celebrate a success ritual. Celebrate the successes in your own life— the finished quilt, the new job, the new skill, the promotion. We all need to remember to praise God for success, as well as to turn to God for help and healing.

Celebration prayers can be part of your regular meal or part of a night out. We always celebrated report cards with a trip to McDonald's and a simple prayer of thanksgiving. Our girls liked getting flowers for successes, while our son liked ice cream. You don't have to spend money to mark a special occasion, however. Simply set aside some time to celebrate and build prayer into it.

Leader: This is the day that the Lord has made.

All: Let us rejoice and be glad in it.

Leader: We praise you, Lord, for calling us together as family. We celebrate N..., who today (name the occasion or achievement). For this success,

All: We thank you, Lord.

Invite family members to share reasons why they are happy for this person, for example, "Because this scholarship will allow Jon to go away to college." The family responds to each reason with "We thank you, Lord." When everyone has said something, ask them if there are any other small successes for which they would like to thank God. To each, respond "We thank you, Lord."

Leader: We praise you Lord for all good things, and we ask you to keep us ever grateful.

All: Amen.

ON FORGIVENESS

There are certain values without which a family cannot survive. Forgiveness is one of the most important of these. (Ways of celebrating forgiveness are explored in the section on forgiveness prayers, in Part I.) Forgiveness involves asking pardon, being forgiven, and receiving a hug, a kiss, or some other sign of reconciliation. Group hugs, called for at times when the family as a whole is being grumpy and difficult, can help to defuse a tense situation.

Asking forgiveness can be hard. In our family, our young children would leave a note of apology on our pillow. A ritual way of saying "I'm sorry" can be helpful; the following ritual develops symbols to use in asking forgiveness. Use the ritual after a stressful family time or at the beginning of Lent. This is not a time, however, to focus on the needs of one individual in the family for forgiveness—the intent here is for the family to celebrate forgiveness as a whole.

Make a small heart for each member of the family. (These can be made out of craft foam, construction paper, pink sponges, or red felt.) Explain to your

54

family why you feel that this would be a good time to have a family reconciliation celebration. Ask everyone to find a stone to bring to supper that evening. Place a small dish in the middle of the family table, and put the hearts around the dish.

Leader: God, our creator,

All: Have mercy on us.

Leader: God, our redeemer,

All: Have mercy on us.

Leader: God, our sanctifier,

All: Have mercy on us.

Reader: A reading from the book of the prophet Ezekiel (36:24–28): Thus says the Lord, "I will take you from the nations and bring you home. I will pour clean water over you and you will be clean; I shall give you a new heart and put a new spirit in you; I will remove from your body the heart of stone, and give you a heart of flesh. I will put my spirit in you…. You shall be my people and I will be your God."

Have each person read one of the petitions below, putting a stone in the dish as he or she speaks, then taking a heart.

Leader: For the times we are less than patient with each other.

All: Forgive us, Lord.

Person 1: For the times we fail to listen.

All: Forgive us, Lord.

Person 2: For the times we fail to obey.

All: Forgive us, Lord.

Person 3: For the times our words are unkind.

All: Forgive us, Lord.

Person 4: For the times we are untruthful.

All: Forgive us, Lord.

Continue in this manner, adding any spontaneous petitions for forgiveness. When everyone has had an opportunity to speak, all say together…

All: Lord, Jesus Christ, son of the living God, have mercy on me, a sinner.

Leader: Lord, help us to be family, loving and forgiving one another as you have loved and forgiven us. Let our stones be a reminder of the need to seek forgiveness from you and from one another.

All: Amen.

Leader: May the peace of the Lord be with you.

All: And also with you.

Exchange a sign of peace among all the members of the family.

Ask family members to keep their hearts in a visible place in their rooms to remind them to be forgiving. Place the dish of stones in an accessible spot in the house. Invite family members to leave a stone at someone's place at the supper table or on the person's pillow whenever they want to say "I'm sorry" and don't know how. The person who receives the stone lets the offender know he or she is forgiven and puts the stone back in the dish.

CELEBRATION OF A DRIVER'S LICENSE

Getting a driver's license is a giant step toward the adult world in the eyes of most children. This new freedom brings new responsibilities for the child, along with a new set of worries for parents. Ritualizing them, and voicing them in a prayer situation that cannot be interpreted as mistrust or nagging, can be helpful to both parent and child. Just remember that this is an age where children reject "churchiness," so keep it simple.

Work with your teen to create a creed which he can profess and adhere to. A sample creed is given here, but don't hesitate to write your own. Have a special meal to celebrate your new driver, and present him or her with a small gift such as a key chain. (One with a small telephone or a "Call Home" inscription can be a lighthearted reminder of the fact that, as parents, we worry.) End your meal with the following prayer ritual.

Parent: God of all protection, we place N... in your care. We rejoice with her in this accomplishment, and challenge her to live up to this new responsibility.

Teen Driver: (Recite this creed, or one that the young person has
    written...)

I believe that driving a car is a serious responsibility, to myself, to
passengers in the car, to those in other vehicles, to pedestrians,
and to the environment.

I believe that traffic laws have been made for our protection and I
will obey them.

I believe that others have as much right to the road as I do and I
will attempt to always be courteous.

I believe that a car is a means of transportation, not a symbol of
power, and I will use it wisely and share in the responsibility of
being a driver in this family.

I believe that a car is an expense that should be shared justly by
all who use it.

I believe that the less parents know, the more they worry, and I will
try my best to call when I am late and to keep them informed.

Parent: Help us, Lord, to support N... in fulfilling his new
        responsibilities. We ask this in the name of Jesus.

All: Amen.

For Parents

Tonight, Lord, I am afraid.
Afraid for all that can happen
   when I am not there to help;
Afraid of others on the road,
   not as responsible as my child;
Afraid of her getting lost,
   being frightened;
Afraid of the pressure her friends will exert;
Afraid of knowing whether or not
   she has the courage to resist.
And I am lonely.
I will miss the friendly talks
   my taxi service permitted;

I will miss precious moments
    alone with her in the car.
I had not realized they were gift.
Keep her safe, Lord,
    and help me to let her go.

BLESSING FOR A NEW HOME

Moving into a new home or apartment is a moment that cries for ritualizing in the family. When our family built our new home, several friends wanted to give us housewarming gifts. We asked them to start a cutting from one of their plants, or, if they were not "plant people," to give us a tiny plant. It was a simple way to bring our friends with us into our new home.

The first step in blessing a new home is to say goodbye to the old one. Walk through your old dwelling together. Stop in each room, and thank God for the joy that you knew there. Ask your children to share one memory from each room. This process may be sad, but there is a certain amount of mourning that is necessary each time we move on to something new. Acknowledging it and giving it a place to be expressed is psychologically and spiritually healthy.

Bring some water from your old home to use in blessing your new one. (Even if it was not a happy home and you are hoping to begin again, we need to acknowledge both the good and bad memories and bring our hope into this new dwelling.) Place the water in a bowl and use a fern or fir branch for blessing.

Go over the ritual with the family and decide who will be responsible for blessing each room. Give a room to each member of the family. Talk about which room is most important to each of you. One person can be responsible for both prayer and blessing, or, if your children are quite young or your family is quite large, you may want to have adults and older children say the prayers, and younger children perform the blessing.

Gather the family at the front door of your new house.

Leader: Welcoming God, bless our door and help us to keep it open to you. May all who enter feel your peace and your welcome.

Dip thumb in water and trace a cross on the doorframe, saying..."In the name of the Father, and of the Son, and of the Holy Spirit. Amen." If you have a holy water font, cross, or some spiritual object you want to keep by the door, now is the time to hang it. Move to the next nearest room. Say each of the following prayers and perform the blessings in the order most appropriate for your house.

Living Room/Family Room

Leader: Loving God, bless us as we gather in this room to laugh and talk and pray. Teach us to enjoy one another and to find comfort in friends and family who gather here.

Dip the branch in water and shake it over the room in a sign of the cross, saying... "In the name of the Father, and of the Son, and of the Holy Spirit."

All: Amen.

Now continue going through each room of the house, pausing to pray and bless in each, sprinkling water and making a sign of the cross.

Kitchen

Nourishing God, bless all who work here. Let each meal we prepare remind us we are called to be salt for the earth.

Dining Room or Kitchen Table

Ever present God, help us to remember that you are the unseen guest at every meal. Let our conversation be gentle and as life-giving as the food that nourishes us here.

Bathroom

Forgiving God, let this room remind us that you wash away all our sins, that you have given us bodies that hold onto nothing that is not life-giving. Help us to let go of anger and hatred as our bodies let go of waste.

Family Bedrooms

God of peace, bless those who use this room with restful sleep that revives and refreshes. Protect us from nightmares and restless anxiety.

Guest Bedroom

Gracious God, bless all who share our home. Give them restful sleep.

Return now to the living room or family room. If you'd like, place a small statue or picture of the Blessed Mother in that room and say this prayer:

Loving Mother, we choose you as the lady and mistress of our home. Protect it from fire and water, from lightning and storms, from disease and hunger, from violence and untruth, from earthquakes and from sudden death. Bless and protect all who live here. May we fill our lives with kindness and love. Amen.

End your blessing ritual with music, a special dinner, or treat.

FOR A SICK CHILD

Illness is one of the times when we are in most need of prayer and feel least like praying. If there is more than one child in a household, it usually means there will eventually be more than one sick child. This is a time when the importance of laying hands cannot be stressed too much. God transmits healing through our hands; the sick child receives strength through our hands. Above all else, touch is comforting when we are ill.

Lay both hands on your child's head...

Parent: Lord our God, maker of the universe, let your healing power descend on N.... Drive out this illness, let the medicine work quickly and thoroughly, and restore him to health. Take away the pain and give him restful, healing sleep.

All: Amen.

Pray for the sick child at grace before meals, and at morning and evening prayer. In the case of serious illness, invite the parish priest in to administer the Anointing of the Sick. (This is no longer considered a sacrament reserved for the dying.) If your children have grown accustomed to praying when someone is sick, they will not be frightened by the more formal ritual of this sacrament.

60

For a Parent Who Is Sick

When we are sick, it can upset the routine of the family, and cause us worry. This prayer will help us to cope.

Lord,
    today, I cannot move.
Not only am I sick,
    I am worried sick.
I am worried about my job
    and the work that won't get done;
I am worried about the carpool,
    about the piano lessons and the soccer game,
    the meals and the homework,
    and that meeting I was supposed to chair.
The worry, so persistent and nagging,
    drains from my body
    the strength it needs to heal.

Help me to let go;
Help me to let others care for the meals,
    the carpool,
    the homework,
    and me.
Remind me that, for one day,
    the world can go on without me.
Watch over the tasks I must leave undone,
    the children I must leave unattended.
And then, Lord,
    watch over me. Amen.

SUMMER VACATION

Everyone needs a vacation. Even if you are unable to get away, try to set aside some time where you slow down your usual work pace and spend more time with the family. When the children have their long break from school, explain to them that everyone will have more time to "vacation" if they take on more of the family work load during their break. Call a family meeting and decide on an equitable division of labor for the vacation stretch.

Decide what you will do with your vacation. Choose some family games you have wanted to play, or plan family outings to parks or museums that you have not had time to visit. Even if the only time you can set aside is three Sunday afternoons or four Wednesday evenings, plan them as carefully as if the family were going to Europe. Part of the fun of a vacation is the planning.

Begin your vacation with a family ritual. If you are going away, it is probably better to do the ritual the night before you leave. The morning will have its share of distractions and problems. If you are having an "at home" vacation, celebrate the ritual at the beginning of your first planned time together.

Gather some symbols of your vacation: board games, cards, books, flashlights if you are going camping, pails and shovels if you are going to the beach. Put them all together in the middle of a table.

Leader: This is the day that the Lord has made.

All: Let us rejoice and be glad in it.

Leader: Lord, you give us vacations to refresh our spirits. You told your own apostles to come apart and rest awhile. Be present to us as we rest. Watch over us as we travel, and keep us safe. Help us to be more present to each other and to you, to slow down, to know we are loved, and to love you and one another more deeply. Let us return to our work renewed. We ask this in the name of Jesus.

All: Amen.

A litany of thanksgiving follows and should be made up of all the things you plan to do. Here is a sample litany that might be used if you were going camping.

Person 1: For tents and sleeping bags,

All: We thank you, Lord.

Person 2: For campfires and marshmallows,

All: We thank you, Lord.

Person 3: For walks in the woods,

All: We thank you, Lord.

Person 4: For lanterns and coolers,

All: We thank you, Lord.

Person 5: For quiet days and starry nights,

All: We thank you, Lord.

Leader: For camping,

All: We thank you, Lord, and ask you to keep us safe as we journey on this vacation. Bless our time of rest. Alleluia.

Compose this type of litany for the beach, or visiting Grandma, or flying to Europe, or staying at home—whatever the destination of your vacation.

GRADUATION

Graduation, like all special life-cycle events, is an important time for sharing memories. High school graduation, in particular, marks a moment that often is the first step in leaving home and moving on to a more independent life. It needs to be celebrated in a way that enables everyone involved to cherish the memories.

Begin putting together a scrapbook or special box for your children when they start high school. (If they are already in high school, start at this point.) Collect pictures of friends and events throughout the graduate's high school years, and newspaper headlines of important national and international happenings. Ask family members to write down stories and memories of events that are shared with the graduate. If you have some pictures or sample papers from the early grades, scatter them throughout the scrapbook for fun.

This activity will require effort on the part of parents, but it will be well worth it. A record of high school years can be more valuable than a baby book, simply because teenagers are far more interesting. It will also remind parents of all the reasons they love this child during what can sometimes be a difficult period of life.

Give the book a title, such as "High School According to...," or the title of the school's yearbook. Then, when high school graduation arrives, you can present this book to the graduate at a family gathering or dinner, using this ritual to mark the occasion.

Leader: Let us bless the Lord,

All: Now and forever.

Parent: Creator God, maker of the universe, bless N... at this important moment in his life. We thank you and praise you, Lord, for all the joy he has brought into our home, for all that we have each learned through him.

Help N... to treasure the memories and the love we have shared, and to always live in such a way that his life gives you praise. I especially thank you for... (Parent mentions something that has been especially important to him or her about this young person, maybe a particular gift this child has brought to the family.)

All: We thank you, Lord.

Now have each family member mention something special about the graduate, with the response "We thank you, Lord."

Parent: These are some of the memories we have shared. (Child sitting to the right of the graduation person holds up the book.) Take them with our blessing and our love.

The book is then passed all around the table. Each family member makes a small cross on the cover with his or her thumb.

All: (Extend hands over the graduate...)
May the Lord bless and keep you.
May the Lord watch over all your goings and comings,
and grant you peace. Amen.

LEAVING HOME

When a young adult leaves for college or moves out to his or her own apartment, it is a time of transition for the whole family, and deserves attention and celebration. Since this can be a time of very mixed emotions, try to keep the celebration lighthearted and fun. If we laughed a little more when we prayed, I suspect we would all pray a little longer. Let your grown children take with them a memory of happy family prayer.

Put together a box of essentials that will be needed: soap, shampoo, toilet paper, a box of tissues, aspirin or acetaminophen, dust pan and brush, window cleaner, and bubble stuff for blowing bubbles (or some other childhood game). Feel free to invent your own gifts and reasons for giving them, and make them different for different children.

Plan an evening for your celebration. This is particularly necessary when children are leaving for college because their lives start moving at a phenomenal pace during the last few weeks. Set a day for a family supper at least one month in advance, and have everyone contribute to the preparations. Ask your young adult to set aside two hours for the meal and celebration.

The ritual given here is based on one used by Sandra DeGidio in her book *Enriching Faith Through Family Celebrations* (see "Suggested Resources," at the back of this book). Use this ritual after sharing your meal together.

Leader:	Let us bless the Lord.
All:	Now and forever.
Leader:	A reading from the book of Genesis (12:1–3): Yahweh said to Abram, "Leave your family and your father's house, for the land I will show you. I will make you a great nation; I will bless you and make your name great so that you will be a blessing. I will bless those who bless you; I will curse those who slight you. And in you all the families of the earth will be blessed. "
All:	Thanks be to God.
Person 1:	N..., I give you shampoo. Never forget that God loves you so much that every hair on your head has been counted.

Person 2: N..., I give you soap. Never be afraid to get your hands dirty in the service of others.

Person 3: N..., I give you window cleaner. May you always care for your visions and listen to your dreams.

Person 4: N..., I give you this dust pan and brush. May it remind you never to sweep unpleasantness under the carpet, but to pick it up and deal with it.

Person 5: N..., I give you these tissues with the wish that your tears will be few.

Person 6: N..., I give you this aspirin in the hope that there will be less pain than joy on your journey.

Person 7: N..., I give you this bubble stuff and wand in the hope that you will never leave your childhood totally behind.

Parent: N..., We give you the key to the house so that you will know you can always come home.

Parent(s) lay hands on young adult leaving home and say:

As you have been loved, may you love.
As you have been nurtured, may you nurture.
As you have been joy to us, may you be joy to others.
May God go with you and bring you peace.

GETTING ENGAGED

When our first child got engaged, we searched everywhere for some type of ritual that would allow us to mark the importance of the event without doing something that would make our young adults feel uncomfortable. We decided to give them candlesticks with a gentle reminder that their love was to be a light in the darkness. We made a commitment to give them candles on each anniversary of their engagement.

Rather than read Scripture at our little celebration, we decided to write our own scriptures. Each family member wrote one or two stories of memories we shared with the daughter who was getting married. We presented them to her

66

and her fiance as a special way of welcoming him into the family by sharing with him our memories.

Rituals are composed of symbol and story. They do not have to involve formal prayer to possess the ability of turning our minds and hearts toward God and one another. With the engaged couple, gather together for a meal together as a family, and pray...

Lord, we ask that you bless our food,
Never let us forget
   that we are not nourished by bread alone,
   but also by love.
Bless this new love as we welcome N... into our family.
Let the memories and the love we have shared bind us together.

For Parents

Lord, teach us to be a gentle, supportive presence,
   as our children begin this new life and new love.
Let our love be a constant reminder
   of your faithful love for them
   and a model of love for one another. Amen.

DEATH IN THE FAMILY

Family death is almost always a time of great sorrow. For children, it can also be a time of great confusion. Our culture tries to gloss over the reality of death, and in so doing, does not give children (or adults, really) the opportunity to deal with their feelings.

Most children understand direct language far better than they do euphemisms. Therefore, they need to know that their loved one is not "sleeping," and that they have not "passed away." They are dead, and this means we will never see them again in this life. At times of death, we need to reassure both ourselves and our children of Jesus' promise that those who love him will live forever in heaven.

67

Gather family close around you to share prayer and support. Begin by telling them this simple story...

Parent: At the last supper, Jesus said to us that we should not let our hearts be troubled. He knew his disciples would be sad when he died, but he did not want us to be worried or anxious. He said that in his Father's house there were many mansions. Jesus meant that in heaven, there would be room for all of us and that he would be there to welcome us.

Let's take a moment and thank God for the things we loved best about N....

Invite each family member to share something special about the person who died, a characteristic or story. After each, a parent should reflect by saying:

Parent: For N...'s ...(here say whatever qualities were mentioned by family members: kindness, wisdom, a sense of humor, gentleness, and the like),

All: We thank you, Lord.

Parent: Comfort us in our sorrow, Lord, and always help us to cherish N... in our hearts.

All: Amen.

The death of a family pet can be just as tragic in the life of a child. It can be ritualized in the same, simple manner given above.

PART III

RITUALS

FOR SPECIAL

TIMES OF

THE YEAR

ADVENT

Advent, the start of the church's new year, is the perfect time for beginning family prayer traditions. Most of us are looking for ways to focus the children's attention on the spiritual meaning of Advent and Christmas, and prayer rituals are a wonderful way to do this.

Some of the Advent rituals here continue throughout the Advent season; some are a single celebration. Most require about five minutes of careful preparation; this time can make all the difference in how your children react to the ritual. Incorporate the children into the preparation. Choose the rituals that work best for you, and remember to relax and make them fun. The principal idea is to begin a tradition that the children will want to continue, that will reinforce not only their faith, but their sense of family.

ADVENT NEW YEAR'S EVE PARTY

Advent is the beginning of the liturgical year. Just as the Jewish people celebrate Rosh Hashanah as the beginning of their year, celebrating the beginning of the church year offers children a sense of Christian identity.

Plan a new year's party for the Saturday before the first Sunday in Advent, complete with decorations and noisemakers and a special dessert that the children can help prepare. Give everyone in the family a piece of paper for writing new year's resolutions, and a plain envelope. Ask children and adults alike to choose carefully one thing they would like to do better in the upcoming year, then write it on the paper and put it in the envelope. Place a special box or small chest on the table for the resolutions.

At supper time, begin with a simple prayer for the new year. You can make up your own or use the one here.

Leader: Lord, we are beginning a new year. We ask your help to live this year aware of your presence in ourselves and in others, especially in this time of Advent when we prepare to celebrate the memory of your coming into the world.

Leader: Lord, this year, please bless me with... (Here, name a quality or attribute that you would like to acquire or improve on). For this, we pray to the Lord.

71

Response: Lord, hear our prayer and bless our year.

Now, each family member prays for one attribute or quality, such as "patience," with all responding "Lord, hear our prayer and bless our year." This prayer can reflect the resolution in the envelope, or can be something totally different. As the family members pray, they add their envelopes to the box. When everyone has prayed, the leader holds up the box.

Leader: Lord, bless us and our resolutions. Keep us as the apple of your eye, throughout this new year.

Response: Amen.

Place the resolution box in a spot of honor, perhaps on the mantel of the fireplace or on a table in the living room, to remind everyone of their resolutions throughout the liturgical year.

ADVENT WREATH

An Advent wreath is a green, circular wreath with four candles, one of which is lit on each of the Sundays in Advent. This custom became popular in Germany during the 16th century, and was brought to the United States by German immigrants. The Advent wreath symbolizes the many years that the people of Israel waited in darkness for the coming of the Savior, and illustrates our waiting during the Advent season, to once again celebrate Jesus' birth into the world.

You can make an Advent wreath by decorating a Styrofoam or florist's ring with live greens (fir branches are good, but anything that's available in your area will do), along with four candles. The candles on the wreath are traditionally three purple and one pink, but they can all be white or all dark blue, as well. Enhance your wreath with pine cones, ribbons, or other decorations, if desired. You can also purchase ready-made wreaths, so don't let a lack of time or creativity rob you of the opportunity for sharing this tradition.

Plan your Advent wreath ritual for each of the four Sundays in Advent, or for the Saturday evening before. In our house, we always lit the candles on our Advent wreath as part of our grace before meals. And because our children enjoyed this custom, we lit the candles every night, not just on Sunday or Saturday evening.

Here follows a simple ritual for blessing the wreath and for lighting the candles. If you want to celebrate Advent every night, use a line from that week's ritual, such as the opening line. If your family is uncomfortable with the blessing, just do the simple prayer of lighting.

This blessing is done only on the first Sunday of Advent. Before you begin, lower the lights in the room to emphasize the darkness that occurred before the coming of Christ.

Leader: Just as the world waited in darkness for the Messiah, the light of the world, we wait in the ever-darkening days of winter for the coming of Jesus.

Reader: A reading from the book of the prophet Isaiah (9:2–3): The people who walked in darkness have seen a great light; on those who live in a land of shadow, a light has shone. You have brought them abundant joy and great rejoicing.

All: Thanks be to God.

Leader: Lord, bless our Advent prayer. Remind us daily of all who wait in darkness for your coming. Give each of us the courage to make your light shine forth in the world. We ask this in the name of your Son, whose coming we await.

All: Amen.

First Week

One candle will be lit this week.

All: Lord, we gather with all those who waited one thousand years for your coming.

Leader: Come, Lord Jesus,

All: Come and be born in our hearts.

Leader: Isaiah, you promised us a light to shine in our darkness.

All: Teach us to wait in patience and to prepare with joy.

One child is chosen to light the candle each night. This child will also extinguish the candle at the end of the meal, and say to the family...

Child: Carry the light in your hearts.

Second Week

This week, light the first candle and a new one.

All: Lord, we gather with all those who waited two thousand years for your coming.

Leader: Come, Lord Jesus,

All: Come and be born in our hearts.

Leader: John the Baptist, you announced the coming of Jesus,

All: Teach us to wait in patience and to prepare with joy.

Continue the practice of having one of the children light the candles, then extinguish them at the end of the meal, saying...

Child: Carry the light in your hearts.

Third Week

Light the candles from the previous two weeks, along with a new one. If you are using purple and pink candles, the pink one is lit on this Sunday, called Gaudete Sunday, when the readings anticipate the joy of the birth of Jesus.

All: Lord, we gather with all those who waited three thousand years for your coming.

Leader: Come, Lord Jesus.

All: Come and be born in our hearts.

Leader: Joseph, you trusted Mary, supporting and protecting her.

All: Teach us to wait in patience and prepare with joy.

On extinguishing the candles...

Child: Carry the light in your hearts.

Fourth Week

All four candles are lit this week.

All: Lord, we gather with those who waited four thousand years for your coming.

Leader: Come, Lord Jesus,

All: Come and be born in our hearts.

Leader: Mary, you believed, and trusted, and waited on the Lord.

All: Teach us to wait in patience and prepare with joy.

On extinguishing the candles...

Child: Carry the light in your hearts.

JESSE TREE

My children's favorite Advent tradition was the Jesse tree. A Jesse tree is a bare branch that holds symbols of people from the Old Testament who waited and prepared for Jesus. Tradition has it that the love and preparation given the Jesse tree would make flowers burst forth from the branch. This is why a bare branch, rather than an evergreen, is used.

In our family, finding the branch was part of the tradition. This may be difficult in warmer climates, but even Florida has some deciduous trees that lose their leaves briefly. Pot the branch in a vase or planter, using sand and stones to help it to stand erect. Next, plan your decorations, using the list on the pages that follow for symbols of Scripture characters.

You can make the symbols out of cardboard, construction paper, or clear plastic transparency sheets that can be traced and colored with magic marker; aluminum foil, last year's Christmas cards, clay, or dough can also work well. You may want to have your family make all the decorations in one sitting, then hang one on the tree each night throughout Advent as you read the corresponding Scripture story. In our family, we told the story of a character from Scripture, made the symbol, then hung it on the tree; this is the ritual described below. Adapt this, however, to fit the needs of your family.

We saved our symbols from year to year, and as the children got older, we simply read different stories about the character then hung the symbol on the tree. When our children reached high school and college age and were often not around to read the stories, we put a Jesse tree up as part of our Advent "decorations" and occasionally talked about what each symbol meant.

On the following pages, you'll find prominent characters from Scripture, the references to where you can find their stories in your Bible, symbols that represent each person, and a synopsis of their stories. As you work on your symbols, find the passage about that character and symbol in your Bible and read it (or a section from it) aloud, or read the synopsis of each story given here.

PERSON	SCRIPTURE	SYMBOL
Adam and Eve	*Genesis 3:1–24*	*an apple*

God created Adam and Eve and gave them a beautiful garden to live in. They were allowed to eat anything except the fruit on the tree of knowledge. Adam and Eve did not want to obey God and ate the fruit. God made them leave the garden, but promised that a Savior would come to redeem them.

Noah   *Genesis 6:11—9:17*   *ark or rainbow*

People in the world grew evil and a great flood came to destroy them. God saved Noah and his family by telling Noah to build an ark and bring a male and female of every animal on board. It rained for forty days and nights, and in the end, God set a rainbow in the sky as a promise that the world would never again be destroyed by flood.

Abraham   *Genesis 12:1—13:18*   *camel*

Abraham was called by God to be the father of the chosen people. He left his homeland and journeyed to the land God promised to give him. He was the first person to make a covenant, or agreement, with God.

Sarah   *Genesis 12:1—13:18*   *tent*

Sarah was Abraham's wife. Even though Scripture does not say she heard God's call, she trusted Abraham and went with him. God promised she would have a son, even though she was very old. She laughed when she heard this, and when they had a son, they called him Isaac, "one who laughs."

Isaac   *Genesis 22:1–19*   *ram*

God asked Abraham to sacrifice Isaac. Just as Jesus carried his cross, Isaac carried the wood for the sacrifice up the hill to the altar. But God would not let Abraham kill his son. An angel came and told him to look in the bushes. He found a ram there for the sacrifice.

Rebecca   *Genesis 25:19–34; 27*   *a well*

Isaac met Rebecca by the well of her father. She bore him twin sons, Esau and Jacob. Even though Esau was older, Rebecca knew that God had called Jacob to be the father of the chosen people. She helped Jacob trick Isaac into giving him the blessing usually reserved for the first-born son.

Jacob   *Genesis 28:10–22*   *a ladder*
Jacob had a dream. In it he saw a ladder reaching up to heaven, and angels walking up and down the ladder. When Jacob woke, he decided the place was very holy and consecrated it to God. He also consecrated his life to God and promised God one tenth of all he would earn.

Rachel and Leah   *Genesis 29:15–30*   *a veil*
Jacob was promised Rachel in marriage. After working seven years to earn the marriage, he was tricked by Laban, Rachel's father, and was married to Leah. He worked another seven years to earn Rachel, and these two women gave birth to the twelve sons who became the twelve tribes of Israel. Rachel was the mother of the two favored sons, Joseph and Benjamin, but Leah was the mother of Judah who was the ancestor of Jesus.

Joseph   *Genesis 39—48*   *coat of many colors*
Joseph was favored by his father who gave him a coat of many colors. His brothers were jealous and sold him into slavery to traders from Egypt. In the end, Joseph grew to fame in Egypt and rescued his family from famine, forgiving his brothers.

Moses   *Exodus 20:1–21*   *commandment tablets*
The whole book of Exodus is the story of Moses. As a baby, he was hidden by his mother in the bushes when the pharaoh was killing all the Hebrew babies, and rescued by the daughter of the pharaoh. When he grew to be a man, he led his people out of slavery in Egypt to the promised land. God gave him the ten commandments.

Miriam   *Exodus 15:20–21*   *tambourine*
Miriam was the sister of Moses, and seems to have been both an advisor and a leader of prayer. When the Israelites escaped Egypt, Miriam led them in song.

David   *1 Samuel 16:1–16*   *stringed instrument*
David was chosen by God to be king of Israel when he was still a young shepherd. He grew to be a great king, but sinned against God. He is believed to have written the psalms.

Solomon   *1 Kings 3:4–15*   *crown*
God promised to give Solomon anything he asked and he asked for

great wisdom. Under Solomon, Israel grew and prospered, but he forgot that it was God who was doing all this.

Elizabeth   *Luke 1:39–55*   *small home*

Elizabeth is the mother of John the Baptist. When Mary found out she was pregnant with Jesus, she journeyed to see her cousin Elizabeth. Elizabeth said that the baby in her womb jumped for joy as Mary approached.

Zechariah   *Luke 1:5–25*   *temple or altar*

Zechariah was a priest. He was serving before the altar in the temple when an angel appeared to him and told him he would be the father of John. Both Zechariah and Elizabeth were very old.

Mary   *Luke 1:26–38*   *lily*

An angel of the Lord appeared to Mary and told her that she was to be the mother of Jesus, even though she was not yet married. A lily represents her purity.

Joseph   *Matthew 1:18–25*   *hammer or saw*

Joseph was the carpenter God chose to be the foster father of Jesus. An angel appeared to him to tell him that the child Mary had conceived was the Son of God.

Jesus   *Luke 2:1–20*   *chi–rho*

The chi-rho is a Greek symbol for Jesus, the Christ, drawn like this:

Other persons to include on your tree are:

Ruth	Book of Ruth	anchor (for faithfulness)
Isaiah	Isaiah 11:1–9	lion and lamb
Deborah	Judges 4	tent peg and mallet
Joshua	Joshua 6:1–15	trumpet
Daniel	Daniel 6:17–24	lion

You can also use symbols or names of family members who are waiting for Jesus to come again.

Suggested Ritual

Begin by reading or telling the story of the character whose symbol you will be making. With young children, use sound effects and voice imitations to hold their attention. Have all family members help in making the ornament, then carry it in procession to the Jesse tree. (You can also carry the candles from the Advent wreath, if you'd like.) At the tree, hang the symbol, then join hands together around the tree. Recite the Hail Mary and close by singing "O Come, Emmanuel" or some other simple hymn.

PREPARING THE MANGER SCENE

This series of simple rituals focuses on preparing the manger scene. Take out your manger set from last Christmas. If you don't have one, you can purchase one at a Christian bookstore or a Christmas shop. Or, make a manger out of a shoe box, with figures fashioned out of papier mâché, starched fabric with Styrofoam heads, wire, or clay. (If you are ambitious and talented, you may want to carve a set out of wood, or make a ceramic set!) Try to have a set that children can touch, since playing with the manger scene can be a gateway to prayer.

Mary will be placed in the stable on the first Sunday, Joseph on the second, the donkey on the third, the shepherds and animals on the fourth, and Jesus on Christmas Eve. Decide in advance who will be responsible for adding each figure. If you have three or more children, this is a good time to give *middle* children a special role. Choose the leader and readers for each of the Sundays.

First Sunday of Advent

To prepare: On an empty table, mantel top, or other convenient location, place an Advent wreath, an empty stable, and the figure of Mary. Give the readers a chance to look over their parts, and have a flashlight available for the readers to see in the dark. Lower the lights. Light the first candle on the Advent wreath, or a single white candle.

All: Lord, we gather with the people who waited one thousand years for your coming.

Reader 1: A reading from the gospel according to Luke (1:26–38): God sent the angel Gabriel to a town of Galilee named

Nazareth. He had a message for a girl promised in marriage to Joseph, who was a descendant of King David. The girl's name was Mary. The angel came to her and said:

Reader 2: Peace be with you. The Lord is with you and has greatly blessed you.

Reader 1: Mary was puzzled by the angel's message and wondered what it meant. The angel said to her:

Reader 2: "Don't be afraid, Mary; God has been gracious to you. You will become pregnant and give birth to a son, and you will name him Jesus. He will be great and will be called the Son of the Most High God."

Reader 1: When Mary asked the angel how this could be, he said:

Reader 2: "The Holy Spirit will come on you and God's power will rest upon you. For this reason, the child will be called the Son of God."

Reader 2: Mary said, "I am the Lord's servant. May it happen of me as you have said."

Leader: The word of the Lord.

The appointed child puts the figure of Mary in the stable.

Leader: Mary, teach us how to wait patiently, to work prayerfully, and never to give up hope. We ask this in the name of Jesus, your Son.

All: Amen.

Second Sunday of Advent

To prepare: Put out the figure of Joseph, along with the Advent wreath, manger, and a flashlight for reading. Lower the lights. Light two candles on the Advent wreath.

All: Lord, we gather with the people who waited two thousand years for your coming.

Reader 1:   A reading from the gospel according to Matthew (1:18–21): This is how the birth of Jesus Christ took place. His mother Mary was engaged to Joseph, but before they were married, she found out that she was going to have a baby by the Holy Spirit. Joseph was a man who always did what was right, but he did not want to disgrace Mary publicly. So he made plans to break the engagement privately. Just when he had decided to do this, an angel of the Lord appeared to him in a dream and said:

Reader 2:   "Joseph, son of David, do not be afraid to take Mary to be your wife, for it is by the Holy Spirit that she has conceived. She will have a son and will name him Jesus, because he will save his people from their sins."

Leader: The word of the Lord.

The appointed child puts the figure of Joseph in the stable.

Leader: Loving God, Joseph trusted you when everyone else doubted. Help us to have faith in you even when things are dark and we are afraid. We ask this in the name of Jesus our brother whose coming we prepare to celebrate.

All: Amen.

Third Sunday of Advent

To prepare: Put out the figure of the donkey, along with the Advent wreath, manger, and a flashlight for reading. Lower the lights. Light three candles (one pink, if you are using these colors).

All: Lord, we gather with the people who waited three thousand years for your coming.

Reader 1:   A reading from the gospel of Luke (2:1–5): At that time, the Emperor Augustus ordered a census to be taken throughout the Roman Empire.... Everyone, then, went to register, each to his own home town. Joseph went from the town of Nazareth in Galilee to the town of Bethlehem in Judea, the birthplace of King David. Joseph went there because he was a descendant of David. He went to register with Mary, who was promised to him in marriage. She was pregnant.

Leader: The word of the Lord.

The appointed child places the donkey in the manger.

Leader: Powerful God, you give us the strength we need for all the journeys in our lives. You give us people to help us, just as the donkey helped Mary and Joseph. Let us always be grateful for those who guide our lives. We ask this in the name of your Son, Jesus.

All: Amen.

Fourth Sunday of Advent

To prepare: Put out the shepherds and sheep, along with the Advent wreath, manger, and a flashlight for reading. Lower the lights. Light four candles on the Advent wreath.

All: Lord, we gather with the people who waited four thousand years for your coming.

Reader 1: A reading from the gospel according to Luke (2: 6–12): While they were in Bethlehem, the time came for Mary to have her baby. She gave birth to her first son, wrapped him in cloths, and laid him in a manger. There was no room for them to stay in the inn.

Reader 2: There were some shepherds in that part of the country who were spending the night in the fields, taking care of their flocks. An angel of the Lord appeared to them, and the glory of the Lord shone over them. They were terribly afraid, but the angel said to them,

Reader 3: "Do not be afraid. I am here with good news for you which will bring great joy to all the people. This very day in David's town, your Savior was born, Christ the Lord! And this is what will prove it to you: you will find a baby wrapped in cloths and lying in a manger."

Leader: The word of the Lord.

Each family member adds a shepherd, lamb, or other animal to the manger.

Leader: Caring God, help us to be open to you in our lives. Slow us down so that we will not miss you when you come. We ask this in the name of Jesus, your Son.

All: Amen.

Christmas Eve

To prepare: Place a single white candle in the middle of your Advent wreath. Give a candle to each person present; put out the infant Jesus figure. Also have out the manger scene, a snuffer for the candles, and a flashlight. Lower lights. Light all four candles on the Advent wreath.

All: Lord, we gather with the people who no longer wait because you have come.

Reader: A reading from the gospel according to Luke (2:15-16, 20): Now, when the angels had gone from them into heaven, the shepherds said to one another, "Let us go to Bethlehem and see this thing that has happened that God made known to us." So they hurried away and found Mary and Joseph and the baby lying in the manger.... And the shepherds returned to their flocks, glorifying and praising God.

Leader: This is the gospel of the Lord.

At these words, the appointed child places the baby in the manger. Since this is a great honor, it should be rotated from year to year. Light each person's candle from one of the Advent candles. Next, all gathered light the single white candle from their candles, and the four Advent candles are snuffed.

Leader: Jesus, we carry your light in our hearts.

All: Amen.

83

The activities that follow can help your family keep the focus on waiting for Jesus as your family prepares for Christmas.

PREPARING THE WAY

The message of Advent is to prepare the way of the Lord. Each of us is called to raise the valleys, and lower the mountains, and make the rough ways smooth to prepare a highway in the wilderness for the Lord. It is a message that appeals to children, one which they can easily understand.

Using large newsprint, make a picture of a highway with the children. Ask them what things get in the way of preparing for the Lord. Choose symbols to represent those things. For example, if they say "being unkind" you might choose a rock to represent unkindness, based on the saying that "Sticks and stones will break my bones." The symbols do not have to be realistic and you may simply choose trees, rocks, or other obstacles one might find on the path.

Make pictures of the symbols, cut them out, and cover the highway with them. Every time anyone in the family does a good deed, that person secretly removes one of the obstacles on the path. (A word of advice: Make *lots* of obstacles. My children always managed to clear the path in a week.)

STRAW FOR THE MANGER

This is a similar idea to the one above. Set the manger scene up with the manger empty and a small box of straw next to the table. Any time anyone does a good deed, that person quietly adds a piece of straw to the manger. This should be done secretly so that it does not become a competition.

CHRISTMAS CARDS

We send cards to one another on Jesus' birthday because we recognize that we are Christ to one another. This year, talk about your Christmas card list as a family. Discuss the people who have brought Jesus into your lives this year as you address envelopes to them. Make it a family project, with parents writing while children stamp and seal, and everyone sharing stories about the important people in your lives.

CHRISTMAS SEASON

Christmas is filled with traditional activities that stress the sacredness of the season. The suggestions given here are designed to help families focus on the holiness of what they are already doing as they prepare for this feast.

DECORATING THE TREE

Our family lives in a climate where it is possible to have a live Christmas tree. So part of our Christmas festivities always involved searching for a tree and cutting it down. If you use a live tree, this can be a fun family activity, if you are not too fussy about the tree.

Plan a particular day to visit the tree farm, the woods, or to pick out a tree that has already been cut. Choose a day that becomes traditional for this activity, so children learn to reserve this time in their schedules. Celebrate finding the tree with hot chocolate and Christmas cookies, and tell stories about other Christmas trees in the children's lives and your own.

Don't be in too much of a hurry to put the tree up, especially if your children are young. Take the time to celebrate Advent without letting Christmas creep in too quickly; a Jesse tree can make the waiting a little more bearable. If you are going to make decorations, use the weeks before Christmas to do so. Cranberries and popcorn can be strung throughout Advent. Other materials for ornaments can be left where children can reach them and work on them during this time as well.

Think about decorations for your Christmas tree throughout the year. Keep souvenirs from family outings, vacations, and special events that can be hung on the tree to help tell your family story. Small school pictures can be mounted on a jar or bottle top (baby food jars are perfect). Spray paint the top, add the picture to the inside, sprinkle glitter on the outside, and glue a fancy ribbon around the edge, leaving a loop on top for hanging. These ornaments become a record of your family's life.

Decorating the tree is very like celebrating Eucharist. We gather, usually with some good Christmas music in the background. We have symbols of our lives together—the ornaments—and, like all our best symbols, they are fragile and need to be handled with care. They are often a little tattered from years of wear, but so are we.

85

Our ornaments each have their own stories. There are the ones each of the children made in kindergarten and scouts, the ornaments their grandmother made that contain pictures from when the children were small, the ornaments their deceased aunt made as a wedding present for us.

There is the glass angel my friend gave to Becky the year Becky was not feeling very good about herself. The angel, Ellie said, was fragile and beautiful, just like Becky. There is the pine cone raccoon that Jon received from a girl he still refuses to identify, and the ribbon angels Liz made when she was trying to raise money to go to Europe. Some of the ornaments are from our families of origin, and we share why they were special to the children's grandparents. We tell our stories, just as we do in Eucharist. We remember our living and our dead.

When the tree is finished, we share a special food (popcorn, in our house), our communion. Then we lower the lights and light the tree and take a few moments to reflect on its beauty.

Decorating a tree is a sacred family act. It requires no special prayers in order to be that, it simply requires we recognize the importance and holiness of what we are doing. As you say goodnight to the children, take a moment to tell them individually what a beautiful ornament they are on your family tree and how grateful you are to God for all the happy memories they have helped to shape. This is definitely a night for a blessing, so check under Evening Prayers for one that fits your children.

CHRISTMAS BAKING

Baking can be a wonderful family activity, and Christmas cookies and breads make great gifts for family and friends. Pumpkin, zucchini, brown, and raisin breads can be baked in a coffee can, covered with the plastic lid, and tied with a ribbon. Even young children can cut and frost Christmas cookies for a gift.

This is a good time for telling the Christmas story, and for sharing family traditions along with family stories about earlier Christmases. When I was growing up, my grandmother always traced a cross on the top of each loaf of bread that she made, and said one Hail Mary when the first sheet of cookies went in the oven. This is a wonderful time to begin to teach children the value of asking God's blessing on the work of our hands.

Save cards from previous Christmases, cut out the pictures, and use them for writing messages with your gift of food. Don't be afraid to tell people that you are giving them a gift on Jesus' birthday because they have made Jesus present in your life this year, and tell them how.

CHRISTMAS EVE

Many churches now offer an evening liturgy on Christmas Eve. The only problem with this Mass is that it is frequently crowded and noisy with overtired children. Encourage your parish to offer two early evening celebrations. This puts Jesus clearly before Santa and the gifts. It gives the family a chance to reflect prayerfully on the real meaning of Christmas.

If you are not in the habit of praying together as a family, Christmas Eve offers a wonderful opportunity to begin. After the children are ready for bed and the stockings have been hung (if you hang stockings), gather everyone in the family or living room. Lower the lights and read the story of the first Christmas from Luke 2:1–20. If you have a manger scene, you can put the infant in the crib at this time. Alternate the honor of carrying the baby to the manger among the children. (I am a middle child, and I still resent family rituals that always have the oldest or the youngest given the most special task!) Use the simple prayer from the Advent wreath ritual, or make up one of your own.

CHRISTMAS CANDLE

A small votive candle (the kind used under warming pots) can be lighted as part of your Christmas Eve prayer and placed in the window to announce that our hearts are ready and waiting for Jesus. Once the baby is placed in the manger, light the candle, saying:

Parent: Lord, we are ready and waiting.

Response: Come and be born in our hearts.

The candle is then carried to a window sill in the front of the house where it can burn *safely* overnight. (Put the candle in a small dish or votive light holder to keep it from burning onto the sill; make sure that the candle is not near curtains or other window coverings.)

CHRISTMAS BLESSING

Christmas Eve is a wonderful time to begin the habit of blessing your children, if you are not doing that already. This blessing can be given as each child leaves the room or as you tuck them in. Place both hands on the head of each child, saying...

> May the Lord watch over your sleeping and your waking,
> And may God bless you (tracing a cross on the forehead with your thumb) in the name of the Father and of the Son and of the Holy Spirit. Amen.

CHRISTMAS MORNING

Christmas morning begins a day of festivity and joy. We found that morning prayer was far more effective and prayerful if we waited until we were sitting down for breakfast, but you may want to pray with the children in their rooms before they come to the tree. Try saying the children's usual morning prayer aloud together. If you have not gotten into the habit of morning prayer, this would be a good time to start. Check the section on Morning Prayer and choose one that is appropriate for your family.

Carry the votive candle that has burned all night to a place of honor on the dining room table. My children always liked to make a procession out of everything. If yours are young, they may want to walk together and sing while they are doing this. If rituals are introduced early enough, even though we may feel strange doing them, the children will perceive them as natural and normal and will have fun with them.

CHRISTMAS DINNER

Since this is a special meal, it deserves a special prayer. Give each person in the family a role in preparing the meal and bringing it to the table. It enhances their self-worth and ownership in making this a peaceful family meal, and eventually (not while they are young, but eventually) it will save stress on the principal homemaker and cook in the family.

Place some candles on the table. You might want to save your Advent wreath, add new candles, and decorate it for Christmas. This helps to symbolize Jesus coming as light into the darkness of our Advent waiting. When everyone has gathered, have a parent or older child read the following Scripture passage (you may use your family Bible or this translation).

Reader: A reading from the gospel according to John (1:1–5):
In the beginning was the Word.

The Word was with God
and the Word was God.

He was in the beginning with God.

All things came into being through him,
and without him not one thing came into being.

What has come into being in him was life,
and the life was the light of all people.

The light shines in the darkness
and the darkness did not overcome it.

Light the candles on the table.

Parent: Come, Lord Jesus.

Response: Come and be born in our hearts.

Join hands and recite your usual grace before meals, or a special grace that someone in the family has composed for the occasion.

HOLY FAMILY SUNDAY

The feast of the Holy Family is celebrated on the Sunday between Christmas and New Year's Day. In the years that Christmas falls on a Sunday, the feast is not celebrated. Some parishes draw attention to this feast by having couples renew their marriage vows at Mass on that day.

This is an opportunity for celebrating your own "holy family." Plan a family activity, whether a visit to other family members, a game, a family movie, or something else your family particularly enjoys. Perhaps the children could take turns each year planning a special activity for this day. Take time to explain to your children that this is a "family" day in your house because it is the day when the church celebrates the family of Jesus and all our families. Make it a traditional fun day, one the children will anticipate each year.

EPIPHANY

The word "Epiphany" means to make manifest. The feast of the three kings is called by this name because this is when Jesus was made manifest, or known, to the Gentiles, to the whole non-Jewish world of which we are all a part. This day is often called little Christmas, and in many European cultures, it is the traditional day for gift-giving. In the new liturgical year, it is celebrated on the Sunday after New Year's Day.

Remembering the Three Wise Men

On the evening of Christmas Day, before bedtime, read the following passage paraphrased from Matthew 2:1–2:

> After Jesus had been born at Bethlehem, some wise men came to Jerusalem from the east. "Where is the infant king of the Jews?" they asked. "We saw his star as it rose and we have come to worship him."

Tell the children the story of how the three kings traveled from far away following a beautiful, huge star in the night sky. Have the children place the statues of the three kings a great distance from the manger scene, on the opposite side of the room, if possible. The wise men are looking for Jesus, and it will be the role of everyone in the family to help them find him.

At supper each day from Christmas to Epiphany, ask who has seen Jesus "made manifest" in someone today. Has anyone in their lives acted in a way that makes Jesus truly visible? Anyone who can share something can move one of the three kings a little closer to the manger. If you saw Jesus in more than one person, you may move more than one king or have a second turn to move all three.

On the actual day of the Epiphany, move all three kings into the manger scene, if they are not already there. Celebrate this feast by writing the names of the three wise men in chalk above the front door. You can incorporate this custom into your meal blessing with a ritual. Begin by placing a piece of chalk on the center of the supper table.

Leader: We thank you, Lord, for the people who have made you manifest to us in these days since Christmas.

Invite the children to say the names of any people they have mentioned in the previous days as making Jesus manifest.

Child: For N…, who made Jesus manifest by…

Family: We thank you, Lord.

After everyone has had a chance to speak, gather at the door of your home.

Leader: Open our hearts and our home, Lord, to all who would
make your presence felt in our lives.

A parent or child takes the chalk and above the door writes $19 + C + B + M + 9$…. The numbers represent the year, the letters, and the names of the three wise men, Caspar, Balthasar, and Melchior. They remain there until the next year. Now return to the table, and say your grace before meals or this prayer…

All: Bless our food and our family, Lord, and keep us ever
aware of your presence among us. Amen.

At supper on the feast day, have a small gift wrapped beside each person's plate. This should not be a gift that was requested, but one that represents each child's special gifts: sheet music for the child who plays an instrument, a special bookmark for the child who loves to read, a batting glove for the baseball player. This gift should not be expensive, just a reminder of each child's specialness, and the fact that we make Jesus manifest through our gifts.

VALENTINE'S DAY

Valentine's Day gives us a wonderful excuse for expressing our love for one another. Put a bare branch in a pot held up with sand, stones, or marbles. The day before Valentine's Day, give everyone some red construction paper and string, and encourage each person to make paper hearts for all the people they love. Write the names of these people on the hearts.

For your blessing before supper that night, let children hang their hearts on the tree, asking God's blessing on each of the people they love, for example, "Thank you, God, for Grandma." Older children may want to include why that person is special. "Thank you, God, for Grandma, who always remembers us with cards and phone calls." Put a heart at each person's place, and on it write why you love that person in a special way. Have the children read their hearts, then hang them on the tree as part of grace before meals.

LENT

Lent is the traditional Catholic time for making sacrifices and doing good works. It is strongly bound up with our understanding of what it means to be Catholic. Lent begins with ashes and ends with palms, two of the most visible signs of our Catholicism. It is an excellent time for developing practices of family piety, as well as for teaching children the true meaning of Lent, and how this fits in with being a Catholic.

Lent comes from the German word for spring. In the early church, it was the time of the immediate preparation of the catechumens—those who were to be baptized—for their full reception into the church at Easter. It eventually came to be celebrated by the whole Christian community as they fasted, repented, prayed, and prepared with the catechumens. It is as important to share this sense of celebration of recommitment and new life with our children as it is to share the meaning of true repentance.

Talk with your family about what it means to "give up something for Lent." Perhaps there are bad habits that need to be changed and could be "given up." Practices such as fasting or giving up something, should be done in conjunction with almsgiving in order to reflect the true intent of lenten denial. Most parishes participate in the Rice Bowl collection during Lent, which helps families focus their fasting on giving to those who have less. Keep a Rice Bowl on your dining room table. Give up candy, then put the money that would have been spent on it in the Rice Bowl. Our family has always had pizza on payday (every other Friday); during Lent, we give that up and place the money in the Rice Bowl.

Consider doing something simple for one another or something for the community, like volunteering at the library or at a soup kitchen. Help children to consider personal works, as well as promises to be made by the family as a whole. Stress the importance of more quiet time and prayer time in Lent, perhaps by having a quiet evening each week when there is no television or stereo.

Read through the various rituals suggested in this book. Which ones will appeal to your children at their present ages? Which ones will be able to become traditions in your family? Which ones have the possibility of leading family members to a deeper understanding of their own faith?

MARDI GRAS

Mardi Gras means "fat Tuesday," and is celebrated on the Tuesday before Ash Wednesday. In the early church, this was the time to finish the meat and butter and eggs before the time of lenten fasting began. Today, a whole week of festive parties precedes Lent in many countries. Plan a Mardi Gras party for your family on the evening before Ash Wednesday.

In England, Mardi Gras was celebrated as shrove Tuesday, or "pancake Tuesday." Pancakes provided a good way to use up the remaining milk, butter, and eggs before the Lenten fast. Even if you do not fast from all animal products in Lent, pancakes for supper the evening before Lent begins can be a strong reminder of the essence of the lenten season. They can be the traditional staple of your Mardi Gras party.

Here are two possibilities for turning supper on the Tuesday before Ash Wednesday into a party.

1. A special dessert, party hats, an "alleluia" sign, and noisemakers can make an ordinary dinner into a party. Prepare a box, covered with purple paper with a foil cross on top. Eat your meal, sing a party song, and welcome in Lent with noisemakers. At the end of the meal, "bury" the noisemakers and the alleluia sign in the box.

Keep the box in a place of honor throughout Lent to remind us that we have set partying aside for this special time. Open the box with a party and an alleluia song on the night of the Easter vigil or at a sunrise Easter celebration.

2. On small sheets of paper, write suggestions for actions to give up during Lent, such as "whining," "arguing," "not listening," or "bothering people who are on the phone." If your children are old enough, ask them to help decide on these actions. Make more than enough for each member of the family with a few left over. Buy purple and pink balloons for your party, or just use a bag of different colored balloons.

Place one of the slips of paper in each balloon, blow it up, and hang it in the kitchen or dining room for the party. String some streamers to make the atmosphere complete.

Close your supper that night with the following prayer service, to lead your family into a time of quiet and repentance.

Leader: God of feasting and God of fasting, walk with us as we journey into Lent.

Reader: A reading from the prophet Isaiah (58:6–7):
The Lord says,
"This is the fast that I choose:
    to loose the bonds of injustice,
    to undo burdens,
    to let the oppressed go free and break all their bonds.
Share your bread with the hungry,
    bring the homeless poor into your house,
    cover the naked,
    and do not hide from those who need you."
The Word of the Lord.

All: Thanks be to God. Alleluia, alleluia, alleluia.

If you are using balloons, now is the time for each person to take one, break it, and read their task for Lent. If you are using noisemakers, have everyone shout the alleluia response and rattle the noisemakers, then place the noisemakers and the "alleluia" sign reverently in the box.

Leader: God of feasting, God of fasting, help us to live out the promises we have made for this holy season.

Response: Hear us, O Lord.

Leader: God of feasting, God of fasting, help us be kind to one another throughout this holy season.

Response: Hear us, O Lord.

Leader: God of feasting, God of fasting, help us find space for quiet each day where we can listen to you.

Response: Hear us, O Lord.

Leader: God of feasting, God of fasting, keep us mindful of the poor.

Response: Hear us, O Lord.

If you have streamers, as each response is made, take down another streamer and cut it into small pieces, dropping the pieces into a special plate or bowl. When you finish the petitions, the atmosphere of the room will have changed from party to repentance.

Leader: God who calls us both to feast and to fast, help us to grow closer to you and to one another through this lenten fast. Teach us to forgive others as you have forgiven us. Call us all to new life in the resurrection of your Son. We ask this in the name of Jesus.

All: Amen.

ASH WEDNESDAY

The traditional fare for breakfast on both Ash Wednesday and Good Friday is hot cross buns. These are made from a sweet dough laced with citron and raisins, and a simple white frosting cross on top. The cross reminds us of Jesus' death and the true meaning of Lent, while the raisins and citron remind us of the sweetness that can be found in fasting and repentance. Although children certainly need to eat more for breakfast than a sweet bun, hot cross buns can be included as part of your Ash Wednesday breakfast. They are usually available packaged in grocery stores.

When we were children, we attended a simple blessing of the ashes and walked up to have ashes placed on our foreheads. The blessing of the ashes is now part of the liturgy and happens right after the gospel. If it is not possible for your family to attend church on Ash Wednesday, you can still participate in this ritual gesture in your home.

Save your palm branches from the previous year's Palm Sunday liturgy. Cut the palms into small pieces, and place them in a small baking dish or ash tray which can sustain the heat of a flame. If you had a Mardi Gras party, you can burn the torn-up streamers and the papers with something to give up for Lent, as well. Burn these as part of the simple prayer service that follows.

Ash Wednesday Prayer

Leader: Let's take a moment and think about something that would help us become holier this Lent. It may be to forgive an old hurt, to be more patient, to share more, or to listen more. Let's make a promise to do just one thing differently this Lent.

If your family members are old enough to write, you may want to ask them to write that one thing down, roll it in a ball, and add it to the dish with the palms, before burning.

Leader: Lord, let our prayer rise as incense.

Leader lights the palms and paper. Be careful. If you have a fireplace, it is a good idea to set the dish in it while it burns.

Leader: We offer you our failings, our mistakes, our goodness, our virtues. Bless these ashes, Lord. Let them remind us of our need to be transformed from ashes to new life.

The leader takes the cooled-off dish, takes a tiny amount of ash and places it on his or her head, or the back of the hands, making a tiny cross with the ash. Each member of the family is then invited to do the same, saying...

Teach me to follow the way of your cross.
Bring all of us to new life in you.

After all members of the family have ashes, join hands, arms, whatever is comfortable for you as a family.

Leader: Help us to grow in love for you and for one another.

All: Amen.

When you bless the children before bed this evening, say...

May God bless you and keep you,
and give to all of us a holy lenten season.

LENTEN CROSS OF CANDLES

This activity echoes the Advent wreath, and offers a simple way to mark the Sundays of Lent. Make your cross by cutting a one-foot log, roughly 5 inches in diameter, in half lengthwise so that it will lie flat on the table. (Friends of ours save a small portion of the trunk from their Christmas tree and make a lenten table cross out of it.) You can also use two pieces of wood from the lumber yard if a log is not available.

Cut four inches off one of the two pieces. This will be the horizontal cross-piece. Notch both pieces so that one can lie flat on top of the other. Drill six holes in the cross for candles and place five purple candles and one pink candle in them (the pink candle will be lit on the fourth Sunday of Lent).

The following prayers can be used for lighting the candles or as part of lenten grace. The first five prayers are based on the gospel readings from Cycle A; these references are given if you want to read these passages from your bible before lighting the candles. The sixth week's prayer is based on the passage about Jesus' triumphal entry into Jerusalem.

Alternate the lighting of the candles and the reading of the prayers between parents and children from week to week, to give each family member a chance to participate.

First Sunday of Lent (Matthew 4:1–11)

Leader: Lord, by your cross and resurrection you have set us free.
All: You are the savior of the world.

Light one purple candle.

Leader: Just as Jesus was led into the desert by the Spirit, help us to listen to the same Holy Spirit, and to be faithful to our lenten prayer and sacrifice.
All: Amen.

Second Sunday of Lent (Matthew 17:1–9)

Leader: Lord, by your cross and resurrection you have set us free.
All: You are the savior of the world.

Light two purple candles.

Leader: Just as Jesus was transfigured before his disciples, help us to be transformed by our lenten prayer and sacrifice.
All: Amen.

Third Sunday of Lent (John 4:5–42)

Leader: Lord, by your cross and resurrection you have set us free.
All: You are the savior of the world.

Light three purple candles.

Leader: Let our lenten prayer and sacrifice become streams of living water that well up inside of us, refreshing us.

All: Amen.

Fourth Sunday of Lent (John 9:1–41)

Leader: Lord, by your cross and resurrection you have set us free.

All: You are the savior of the world.

Light four purple candles.

Leader: Just as Jesus cured the blind man, may our Lenten prayer and sacrifice give us new vision.

All: Amen.

Fifth Sunday of Lent (John 11:1–45)

Leader: Lord, by your cross and resurrection you have set us free.

All: You are the savior of the world.

Light four purple candles and one pink candle.

Leader: Just as Jesus called Lazarus from the dead, may our lenten prayer and sacrifice lead us to new life.

All: Amen.

Passion (Palm) Sunday (Matthew 21:1–11)

Leader: Lord, by your cross and resurrection you have set us free.

All: You are the savior of the world.

Light all the candles.

Leader: Hosanna to the son of David. Blessed is he who comes in the name of the Lord.

All: Amen.

ALLELUIA CROSS

An alleluia cross is a simple way to remind everyone to pray, make sacrifices, and do good deeds throughout Lent. I first saw one made at Guardian Angels parish in Rochester, New York.

Make a large black paper cross to hang on a wall, on the refrigerator, or any place where it will be seen all the time and where everyone in the family can reach it. Using colored construction paper, or white paper and magic markers, make brightly colored mosaics (simple block designs) that can be taped or glued to the cross. You can also make these mosaics at your Mardi Gras party, from the streamers that were hung for decoration.

Every time someone makes a sacrifice for Lent or does a good deed in secret for someone, that person can add a colored piece to the cross. Decide among family members what constitutes a good deed; it should be something out of the ordinary that requires real effort. If you want to make this more of a family project, the horizontal piece of the cross can be reserved for good deeds the family decides to do together. Try to have a total mosaic cross by your Easter celebration.

PRETZELS

During the Middle Ages, pretzels were considered a lenten bread because they were made without butter or animal fat. The shape of the pretzel represents praying arms. Choose one night in Lent to make pretzels. Use pizza dough that you buy from the supermarket. Cut the dough into strips of about 8 inches, roll the dough into ropes, and shape the ropes into pretzels. Place these on a baking sheet or plate, then cover with a dish towel and let rise for 45 minutes.

In a non-aluminum pan, bring 4 cups of water and 5 teaspoons of baking soda almost to a boil. Using a slotted spoon, place the pretzels carefully in the water for approximately one minute, turning once. Do not let the water come to a boil. Remove pretzels and place on a greased baking sheet. Sprinkle with coarse salt (sea salt or Kosher salt) and bake at 425 degrees for about 12 minutes. After removing the pretzels from the oven, say this simple prayer over them...

> Lord, let these praying hands
>   remind us to be faithful
>   to our lenten prayer and sacrifice.

Use pretzels for a snack during Lent, repeating the prayer before eating them. Pack them in your children's lunches, to remind them of the lenten season. If you do not want to go to the trouble of baking pretzels, buy a box of pretzels from the store, bless them, and use them in snacks and lunches.

LENTEN CALENDAR

A lenten calendar is similar to an Advent calendar, except that it tells the events leading up to the passion and death of Jesus, rather than his birth. You'll be hard-pressed to find a lenten calendar in the store, so plan to make one. Start with a large picture, preferably a religious scene that will remind everyone of Lent. We used maps of the Holy Land in Jesus' day so that the children could see the places where Jesus lived and ministered.

Cut forty windows in the picture, and number the windows on the front. Once the windows are cut, paste the picture to a plain white backing. Behind each window, on the backing, put a Scripture reference. The references should tell the story of the public life of Jesus, ending with the passion, death, and resurrection. Let a different family member each night open the window and read the Scripture.

The following references tell the story of the public ministry of Jesus in the order given by the synoptic gospels. If you use a map of the Holy Land for your picture, some suggestions are given on where to place a particular window. (These are rough suggestions; don't be afraid to place the window in some other spot, particularly if the Scripture reference does not name the place.)

1. Mark 1:9–11 (put on a window by the Jordan river, near the Dead Sea)
2. Luke 4:1–13 (in the desert beyond the Jordan)
3. Luke 4:16–19 (Nazareth)
4. Mark 1:16–20 (Sea of Galilee)
5. John 1:43–51 (Sea of Galilee)
6. John 2:1–12 (Cana)
7. Mark 1:21–28 (Capernaum)
8. Mark 1:29–31 (Capernaum)
9. Luke 4:42–44 (just outside Capernaum)
10. Mark 1:40–45 (north of Capernaum in Galilee)
11. Mark 2:1–12 (general area of Capernaum)
12. Mark 3:7–12 (hill country northwest of the Sea of Galilee)
13. Mark 4:1–9 (on Sea of Galilee, near east shore)
14. Mark 4:35–41 (middle of Sea of Galilee)
15. Mark 5:1–20 (east side of the Sea of Galilee)
16. Mark 6:1–6 (Nazareth)

17. Mark 6:7–13 (outside Nazareth)
18. Mark 6:17–29 (Tiberias)
19. Mark 6:30–44 (southwest of Sea of Galilee)
20. Matthew 5:1–12 (northwest of Sea of Galilee)
21. Mark 7:24–30 (Tyre)
22. Mark 7:31–37 (northern Decapolis region)
23. Mark 8:22–26 (Bethsaida)
24. Mark 9:2–8 (Mount Tabor)
25. Luke 9:51–56 (Samaria)
26. John 4:1–30 (Samaria)
27. Luke 10:38–42 (Bethany)
28. Luke 11:1–4 (northeastern Judea)
29. Luke 15:1–7 (outside Jerusalem)
30. Luke 19:1–10 (Jericho)
31. Luke 19:28–38 (Jerusalem)
32. Luke 19:41–44 (Jerusalem)
33. Luke 19:45–48 (Jerusalem)
34. Luke 21:1–4 (Jerusalem)
35. John 2:14–16 (Jerusalem)
36. Luke 22:1–6 (Jerusalem)
37. Luke 22:14–20 (Jerusalem)
38. Luke 22:39–46 (Mount of Olives)
39. Luke 22:47–53 (Mount of Olives)
40. Luke 22:54–62 (Jerusalem)

The calendar will be completed at the beginning of Holy Week. The remainder of the passion, found in Matthew 26:14—27:66, Mark 14:1—15:23, or Luke 22:14—23:56, can be read during Holy Week.

LENTEN ALTAR

When I was a child, we always made May altars. We would cover a box with a linen napkin, place a statue of Mary on it, and keep fresh flowers in front of her throughout the month. I remember those altars vividly; they were very important. With my own children, we created altars for different seasons. One particular table in the living room became the site for our altars, and the altars became silent reminders of the liturgical season.

A lenten altar can take many forms. Ours usually emphasized that Lent was the season in which the catechumens prepared for their baptism into the church. We would put each child's baptismal candle and robe on the table, with a small card showing the date of baptism and a few pictures. A crucifix was placed at the center of the altar, and a small picture of our parish church was beneath it. If the parish had given us anything as part of our lenten journey (and we have received everything from egg timers to railroad spikes), those things would also be on the table.

There are many other themes that can be used as well. A desert theme could be used to focus on the idea of coming to a quiet place to pray, using a cross, sand, stones, and a few cactus plants. A bible can form the center of a liturgical altar, with symbols added from each of the six weeks' gospels. Invite the children to listen carefully to the Gospel each Sunday morning, then decide on a new symbol to add to the altar. Use your imagination and input from family members in creating a lenten altar that is meaningful for your home.

HOLY WEEK

Holy Week contains the most important celebrations of the church year. Because of this, it has always puzzled me that the Triduum (Holy Thursday, Good Friday, and Holy Saturday) have not been made holy days of obligation. Whether or not you are able to celebrate with the larger church community on these days, they are rich in symbolism and offer families the opportunity to celebrate rituals at home.

PASSION (PALM) SUNDAY

Passion Sunday is one of the liturgical feasts people are most apt to remember from childhood. The concrete symbol of palms impressed us; the long gospel was a reminder of the importance of the day and of the week that was beginning. As we celebrate this feast with our children, it is important to stress that we are remembering what Jesus did, not re-enacting these events. We are an alleluia people, who know that our story will end in resurrection.

The people of Jesus' day grabbed branches off nearby trees to wave before him. If Jesus had lived in a cold, northern country rather than the desert of

Palestine, people would have grabbed fir branches rather than palms. Although palms are readily available in some sections of this country, it would be appropriate for people to use whatever branches are native to their area for the Passion Sunday celebration.

If you live in a colder area, try bringing in forsythia branches and putting them in warm water a few weeks ahead of time, forcing them to blossom earlier. Try a few branches at several different times so that you will be sure to have some blossoming for Passion Sunday. Bring the branches to church with you on Passion Sunday, as a sign of what you actually have available to welcome Jesus.

If you know someone who is good at fashioning crosses from palm, ask her or him to show you how. With your palms from church, make crosses and visit a shut-in, bringing your crosses as a gift. Children can sometimes feel awkward on visits to the sick and elderly. Having something to bring is helpful and the shut-ins will be thrilled with the visit.

Make a centerpiece for the table with palms and your own branches. You might want to take the donkey from your Christmas crèche and add it to the centerpiece. It will serve throughout the week as a reminder of Jesus' passion, and can be replaced with Easter eggs and new life decorations for Easter Sunday.

HOLY THURSDAY

There are two different versions in the gospels about the Last Supper. Matthew, Mark, and Luke tell one version, about the first celebration of the Eucharist. John's gospel does not mention the Eucharist: He simply tells the story of the washing of the feet. The emphasis in John's gospel is on service; the emphasis in the synoptic gospels (those of Matthew, Mark, and Luke) is on community.

Jesus wanted to make sure that he would be remembered, that he would continue to live in the minds and hearts of his people. Use the following ritual during your meal on Holy Thursday to show the importance of remembrance and of community in our lives as Christians.

Ask all members of the family to bring a souvenir to the supper table that reminds them of a special time, place, or person in their lives. Place an unsliced loaf of bread at the center of the table (if it can be homemade, all the better). Add grapes, a special cup for wine or grape juice, and wheat stalks, if you are able to get some. If you have older children, one of them might enjoy acting as leader for the prayer service; have them prepare ahead of time.

At your grace before supper, ask each person to thank God for the memory that their souvenir calls to mind. Go around the table, and have each person hold up their item, saying...

Thank you God, for... (e.g., our summer vacation, the basketball game, the school play).

During supper, ask family members why we keep souvenirs and discuss how important it is to each of us to remember special times and places. This is the night to reflect on how we cherish memories in our family. You might want to tell a story during dinner about a particular occasion or event that is of importance to your family.

Place bread and a cup of wine or grape juice before the person who will act as leader.

Leader: The Lord Jesus, on the night before he died, took bread (raise up the loaf of bread) blessed it, broke it, and gave it to his disciples saying: "Take this and eat for this is my body."

Break a piece of bread off, hand it to the person to your left, and say "Peace be with you." Then hand the person the loaf of bread. Each person breaks the bread, hands a piece to another, and then hands the loaf to that person to break. The last person gives a piece to the leader.

Leader: Then Jesus took the cup (leader lifts the cup of wine or juice), gave it to his disciples and said: "Take and drink. This is my blood that is poured out for you."

Pass the cup around the table, allowing each person to sip from it.

Leader: Whenever you do this, do it to remember me.

Prayer: Lord, help us to remember that whenever we gather around the table you are present in a special way. Help us to remember you in all that we do, and to be real presence in each other's lives. We ask this in your name.

All: Amen.

GOOD FRIDAY

There are very few children who grow up in the Christian tradition who don't eventually ask why this day is called good. What we commemorate on this day doesn't seem good: Jesus is condemned by an unjust process, carries his cross to Calvary, and dies. After his death, his body is taken down and laid in a borrowed tomb. What's good about all that?

Good Friday was called that *after* Easter Sunday occurred, after we knew how the story ends. It is a constant reminder to all of us that great good can come out of the worst possible disasters, for what could have been worse in the eyes of the disciples than the death of Jesus?

Christ did not die once and for all. If we believe what St. Paul tells us, we are all part of the body of Christ, who continues to suffer and die in the world around us.

To mark this day, strip your dining room table bare of any placemats, table-cloths, centerpieces, candles, and the like so that it resembles the bareness of the altar at church. Place a plain cardboard or wooden cross at the center of the table and leave it there all day. During the day, ask family members to think about people who are suffering in the world today, then write down their thoughts and bring them to the supper table that evening. You'll need to help your young children with this.

Encourage quiet in the house for the whole afternoon. Keep the television and radio off. While children are not required to fast, keep the meals simple so that they recognize the nature of fasting.

At supper, ask everyone to talk about the suffering person or group of people that each brought to the table. After naming the person or group, tape the piece of paper to the cross in the middle of the table. When each family member has spoken, say this prayer, or one that you have written.

All: Lord Jesus, you continue to suffer in people today. Help us to be aware of the needs of others, and to do all we can to bring peace to our world and everyone in it. Amen.

During the meal, discuss the possibility of doing one thing as a family to relieve someone's suffering.

105

HOLY SATURDAY

This day is one of preparation for Easter. It is rich in symbols that families can use and celebrate in teaching resurrection.

EASTER EGGS

Eggs remind us of the new life that is present for all of us in the resurrection of Jesus. In pre-Christian times, eggs were a symbol of fertility, and people presented them to one another at the beginning of spring. During the Middle Ages, the eating of eggs was prohibited during Lent. So, on Easter morning, Christians would give eggs to one another to celebrate the breaking of the lenten fast. The egg became the symbol of the tomb from which Christ emerged, calling us all to resurrection and new life.

Take time on Holy Saturday to color eggs with your family. If you pierce the shells with a pin and allow the eggs to come to a boil slowly, they are less apt to crack. Eggs can also be blown out by piercing both ends with a pin, covering the hole on one end with a straw, then blowing evenly through the egg. These hollow eggs can be decorated and kept from year to year, and the blown out egg can be used to make breakfast on Easter morning.

While you are coloring eggs, you can share the symbolism of the egg and the story of Jesus' resurrection. The stories from chapters 20 and 21 of John's gospel and from chapter 24 of Luke's gospel will provide ample storytelling material. Read them through yourself and choose one to tell as you decorate the eggs.

NEW LIFE CENTERPIECE

Take a Holy Saturday walk with your family and look for signs of new life. Buds on trees, blossoms, seeds, and cocoons are all signs of life awakening with the spring. Choose some of these symbols to bring back into the house and make a new life centerpiece for your Easter table. Read the Emmaus story from Luke 24:13–35, and relate it to your children as you walk.

EASTER BREAD

Bread can be a wonderful symbol of resurrection for children. The yeast brings the flour to life, just as the Spirit of God brought Jesus back to life. The Spirit is like yeast in all of us, permeating us, helping us to grow. Our family is the warm, moist place that allows the yeast of the Spirit to do its work in us.

Try baking bread with your children on Holy Saturday. A simple white bread, a sweet bread, or French bread are all good choices because they rise so visibly. Most basic cookbooks have simple recipes (I use the recipe for French bread in the Fannie Farmer cookbook). Choose a warm, *dark* place for the bread to rise, such as your oven, to help the children understand the connection with the tomb.

All breads must be kneaded at least once. Although proper kneading is important to the texture of the bread, the bread is less important today than the lesson you are teaching about resurrection. Give each of the children a chance to pound and knead. Explain that for the yeast to be able to act, the bread needs to be pounded down in this fashion. Sometimes we feel like we are being pounded and kneaded. Perhaps we are getting ready for new life in the Spirit.

Talk with the children about any times when there was suffering in their lives and the new life that came out of it. If you want to add raisins or citron to your bread, ask them to remember some of the "sweet moments" that came out of their pain. Bake the bread. Our family and our lives can only help to prepare us for new life in Christ. Ultimately, we must be transformed by God, just as the dough is transformed by the heat of the oven. Enjoy it with your family on Easter morning.

BLESSING OF THE FOOD

Several ethnic groups have kept alive the tradition of blessing food on Holy Saturday. The staples for the Easter Sunday meal (or, in some cultures, the Saturday vigil meal)—bread, wine, the colored eggs, the ham—are all placed in a basket and brought to the church to be blessed. Even if your parish does not celebrate this custom, it is a good one to start with your family.

Place the bread and the eggs, the fresh vegetables and fruit, and whatever beverage you will be having in a basket on the table at dinner on Holy Saturday. Invite everyone in the family to extend hands over the basket, while the leader says:

Bless this food, Lord...

eggs, the symbol of new life,

bread and wine, the sign of your presence with us,

fruit and vegetables, products of the earth

and the new life of spring.

We praise you for the new life

you bring us through your resurrection,

And for your nourishing and sustaining presence

in these, your gifts.

All: Amen. Alleluia!

NEW FIRE/EASTER CANDLE

One of the great symbols of the Easter vigil is the symbol of the new fire. My family likes to make our own Easter candle (also called a Paschal candle), and it is a fitting way for the family to mark the Easter season. To make the candle, use a plain, wide white candle three to four inches in diameter. You will also need five red tacks or five grains of incense to represent the five wounds of Jesus, and some colored contact paper that will stick on the candle. (If you do not want to go to the trouble of cutting out the symbols from the contact paper, bright red nail polish will work very well.)

Cut an *alpha* A and an *omega* Ω out of the paper (these are the letters at the beginning and the end of the Greek alphabet), as well as numerals to represent the year. The numerals and Greek letters could also be scratched on the candle, but the candle is prettier and has more power as a symbol when these stand out. Read through the ritual and decide who will do which parts, and give everyone an opportunity to read it in advance. Prepare a table outside your house on which the candle will stand, and put the letters and numbers in a dish beside it. Set up a fire-resistant dish with kindling or twigs in it on the ground next to the table, or put several coals in a charcoal grill.

Take the family outside to watch the sunset. Explain that each time the sun sets, we remember that Jesus died for us and rose on Easter morning. Return to the house, but do not turn on any lights. When it starts to get dark enough for it to be difficult to see, take everyone back outside for the ritual.

Light a small fire in the fire-resistant dish or grill. While the fire should really be lighted from flint, you can use matches if you do not have a boy scout or girl scout in your family. Gather around the fire in silence, and then pray…

Leader: This is the holy night when Jesus overcame death and rose to new life. We honor the memory of his death and resurrection, knowing that we will rise with him and live forever.

Person 1: Christ yesterday and today (with a toothpick, the person makes a line on the candle to represent the vertical piece of the cross),

Person 2: The beginning and the end (second person makes horizontal arm of cross),

Person 3: The alpha (place alpha on top of cross),

Person 4: And the omega (place omega at the bottom of the cross).

Person 1: All times belong to Christ (place first numeral of the date in the upper left corner of the cross),

Person 2: And all the ages (place second numeral in upper right corner of the cross),

Person 3: To him be glory and power (place third numeral in lower left corner),

Person 4: Down through the ages and forever (place fourth numeral in lower right corner).

The grains or tacks are then inserted, one into each end of the cross, with the fifth in the middle of the cross. As you place each one in, pray these words…

By these holy (place first tack),
  and sacred wounds (place second),
  may Christ our Lord (place third),
  watch over us (place fourth),
  and keep us (place fifth). Amen.

Light the candle from the fire.

$$\begin{array}{c} \text{A} \\ \begin{array}{c|c} 1 & 9 \\ \hline 9 & 5 \end{array} \\ \Omega \end{array}$$

Leader: May the light of Christ rising dispel all darkness from our hearts and minds.

Leader holds up the candle and says...

Leader: Christ, the light in our darkness.
All: Thanks be to God.

The leader then leads the family into the house. In every room, the leader says "Christ, the light in our darkness," to which everyone responds "Thanks be to God." Someone then turns the lights on in that room. When the whole house is lit, the family gathers in one room and sings an Easter song.

Even if your family does not want to celebrate the whole ritual, it is still great fun to walk through the dark house with a lighted candle turning lights on. Create an Easter candle in advance with any symbols of new life—butterflies, flowers, eggs—light the candle outside as it grows dark, and carry it to each room of the house in the manner suggested in the ritual.

EASTER SUNDAY

SUNRISE CELEBRATION

If your family is young and up at the crack of dawn on Easter (and if you live some place where you can actually see dawn), you may want to consider a sunrise celebration. If it is not too cold, plan a picnic breakfast to take with you to a place where you can see the sunrise and enjoy each other's company. Bring bells, or a trumpet, or noisemakers with you. If you "buried" an Alleluia sign and noisemakers at the beginning of Lent, bring the "casket" with you, opening it at sunrise.

The rising sun is the symbol of Jesus' triumph over death. Just as the sun disappears over the horizon each evening and rises again in the morning, Jesus died and rose again. And he promised that we would, too. Easter is a celebration of that promise, as well as a celebration of the resurrection of Jesus.

Ask everyone to wait very quietly for the sunrise, without speaking or moving, just as Jesus waited quietly in the tomb. As soon as someone spots the first rays of the sun, he or she can begin to ring a bell or make noise. All the others join in. As the noise dies down, begin the ritual.

Leader:	This is the day that the Lord has made.
Response:	Let us rejoice and be glad in it.
Leader:	Lord, you give us new life.
All:	Alleluia!
Leader:	Lord, you give us this new day.
All:	Alleluia!
Leader:	Lord, you give us our world and all that is in it.
All:	Alleluia!
Leader:	Lord, you give us each other.
All:	Alleluia!
Leader:	We praise you God, maker of the universe, for sending us Jesus and calling each of us to new life in him.
All:	Amen.

Close with an Easter song, then go home to hunt for eggs, prepare for church, or whatever it is that your family does on Easter morning. If you have an Alleluia sign that was buried at the start of Lent, put it up in the room where you will eat your main meal.

A sunrise service does not have to be celebrated at sunrise, if the early hour is a little daunting for your family. It is still more fun outside, though, if you live in an area where that is possible. Gather the family in the back yard or on the roof of the apartment building and celebrate.

BUTTERFLY BLESSING

Easter is a season of fifty days, the longest liturgical season in the year besides ordinary time. Part of truly celebrating Easter is making the sense of new life last (the way some of us once tried to make the Easter candy last!). This blessing is a way to help your family keep Easter in their hearts and minds.

Butterflies are a symbol of new life. They begin life as simple worms, wrap themselves up in a cocoon, and emerge as beautiful creatures, no longer crawling but flying. This is the life Jesus calls us to as we emerge from the cocoon of Lent.

Have your children make butterflies for your Easter meal, at least twenty of them. Colored tissue rectangles, gathered in the center and wrapped with a pipe cleaner (the two ends twisted together then extending as antennae) are very effective, but cardboard or paper butterflies will do just fine.

On small slips of paper, write messages about what kinds of people are "butterflies," people who know they have been called to fly, to live life differently. For example: "Butterflies always listen when we need them," "Butterflies never fly in people's faces," "Butterflies always look for the sweetness." You can make these expressions as abstract or as simple as you want, depending on the ages of the children. Tape a saying to each of the butterflies and put them in a dish on your Easter table.

Begin your Easter meal with the following blessing...

Leader: This is the day that the Lord has made.

All: Let us rejoice and be glad in it.

Leader: Lord, You call us all to new life.

All: Alleluia.

Leader: Help us to leave the safety of our cocoons and learn to fly.

All: Alleluia.

Leader: (Hold up the dish of paper butterflies...) Show each of us the new life to which we are called.

All: Alleluia.

Leader takes a butterfly, reads the message, and returns it to the dish. Each family member does the same. Parents can read to little ones the message on their butterfly and explain it, if necessary.

Leader: Bless our food, Lord, and help us to experience an Easter season filled with new life.

All: Amen. Alleluia!

Throughout the Easter season, have everyone take a butterfly at breakfast each morning, read the message, and return it to the dish. The prayer can be used each evening at supper, or on Sundays until Pentecost. This prayer can also be used very effectively without the butterflies as a special Easter season grace.

EARTH DAY

Earth day is a wonderful time to help children focus on the way they treat the earth. In New England, where I live, it is still too cold at the end of April to think about yard work or gardening, but in warmer climates this would be an excellent day for a family outdoor cleanup, readying the garden for planting, or preparing a window box or terrace garden.

Plan an Earth Day centerpiece for the table where you eat your main meal. One way to do this is to fill a basket with anything from rocks and plants to fresh fruit and vegetables. At your meal, talk about an "earth resolution" that the whole family can make. Most of us have been recycling for many years now, but there is more that we can do for the earth: Use cloth napkins instead of paper, with children taking turns making sure they are washed and ready; carry sandwiches in reusable plastic containers instead of plastic bags; plan a litter hike or take part in one; join a group committed to keeping one of the city parks clean.

Earth Day offers an excellent opportunity to demonstrate to children that it is not enough to believe in something; we must act on what we believe. The earth is our responsibility. Make your resolution part of a "grace after meals." Choose a fresh fruit for dessert. Begin this Earth Day ritual by asking everyone to think about all the "fruits" of the earth, and how they use and enjoy them.

Parent: We thank you, creator God, for the fruits of the earth; for... (parent mentions any gift the earth gives us and how we use it, such as air to breathe, trees to climb, water to drink and swim in, apples for pie, or ice for skating).

Child: We thank you, creator God, for... (each child thanks God for something the earth has given).

Parent: Creator God,
Teach us to care for the earth you have given,
    never taking what we do not need,
    never destroying its beauty or its power
    with our greed or laziness.
Help us to remember
    we must care for the earth
    if it is to care for us, and for our children's children.
We promise to do our part by... (here each person states what they will do to keep this resolution.)

Child: Help all of us to walk gently on the earth.

All: Amen.

113

PENTECOST

Pentecost is the feast of the Holy Spirit. We picture the Spirit as wind, as breath, or as a gentle breeze. Plan a Pentecost activity that can become a tradition in your family, such as kite-flying or bubble-blowing. This is a good way to teach children how important the Holy Spirit is to our own lives, just as the wind is to kites and breath is to bubbles. Have a picnic to go along with your activity.

Pentecost is a good day to put the wind chimes back outside for the summer. It is the wind of the Spirit blowing through us that makes music for all to hear. Plan a party with balloons. Since Pentecost is considered the birthday of the church, you could include a birthday cake for the church.

Cut out little doves, and on each one write a gift of the Holy Spirit: wisdom, understanding, counsel, knowledge, fortitude, piety, and fear of the Lord (awe). The same thing could be done with the "fruits" of the Spirit, as found in St. Paul's letter to the Galatians (5:22): love, joy, peace, patience, kindness, generosity, faithfulness, gentleness, and self-control. These virtues may be easier for young children to understand than the gifts of the Spirit.

Put the doves in a pretty dish and let everyone take one as part of grace before meals. Let each person make their dove part of a litany. Each person reads the gift they have been given and all respond as follows...

Person: Spirit of understanding,
All: Make me your dwelling.

After everyone has spoken, pray...

Leader: Holy Spirit, you fill our lives. Help us to live as people of your Spirit, gifted and holy.
All: Amen.

After the meal, close with the Holy Spirit prayer.

> Come, Holy Spirit, fill the hearts of your faithful,
> and kindle in them the fire of your love.
> Send forth your spirit
> and they shall be created.
> And you shall renew the face of the earth. Amen.

If you make your doves out of sturdy cardboard, you could then use them to make a mobile to hang over your table during Ordinary time. It is the Holy Spirit, acting within us, that enables us to be good Christians. Making this day a traditional day for a special celebration helps to emphasize the importance of the Spirit in our lives.

MOTHER'S DAY/FATHER'S DAY

It is important for children to understand that a parent is not just someone who is their biological mother or father. A parent is someone who cares for a child and helps him or her to grow.

To mark these two days, have everyone in the family make lists of all the people in their lives who do nurturing things for them. Make little cards for each of them, then send off the cards. If you are not a biological parent, stepparent, or adoptive parent, explain to your children that there are other less traditional parenting roles. You are still mother or father to them, and you would be delighted to celebrate this special day.

Do not let the materialism of the day take possession of your celebration. Tell the children you will leave a list on the refrigerator of all the things you would like to have done as a gift for Mother's Day or Father's Day. Keep it simple and not too demanding, so that children will feel they can accomplish these things and give you your list, with all the chores crossed off, as a gift.

Plan an easy meal that you and your children and/or spouse can fix together. Or plan a picnic in the backyard or a neighboring park. Include, as part of your grace, a special blessing for father or mother (or the person who fills that role in your home).

Child:	Let us bless the Lord,
All:	Now and forever.
Child:	Lord, we thank you for our mother (father, stepmother, uncle, grandmother, or whomever you are celebrating).
	For all the times... (Here, have each child mention something special that his or her parent does.)
All:	We thank you, Lord.

Children then circle around parent and lay hands on her or him while oldest child says...

Child: Lord, our God, bless our mother (father) with your love. Give her (him) wisdom, patience, gratitude, and a sense of humor. Help us to be a family that always supports one another in love.

All: Amen.

FOURTH OF JULY

Independence Day presents a wonderful opportunity for teaching children that part of our responsibility as Catholic Christians is to be good citizens of our nation. Begin the day with a flag-raising event, if possible, holding it before breakfast so that it is the first action of the day. Flags can be purchased fairly inexpensively and can be mounted on brackets on the side of the house or garage, or at the apartment window. There is no need for a true flagpole.

Choose one member of the family to carry the flag to the place where it will be mounted. This is a great honor and needs to be rotated each year among the children. When you reach the appointed spot, form a circle around the child and read a patriotic poem, or part of a famous speech, such as John F. Kennedy's inaugural address, Abraham Lincoln's second inaugural address, or Martin Luther King's "I have a dream" speech. Your local library can probably help you find something appropriate for the ages of your children, and something that challenges them to understand their own responsibility to make their country a land of opportunity for all people.

Start this ritual by mounting the flag, and all saying the Pledge of Allegiance.

I pledge allegiance to the flag of the United States of America, and to the Republic for which it stands, one nation, under God, indivisible, with liberty and justice for all.

Leader: Lord, bless our country and its leaders. Bless our president, N..., our senators, N... and N..., our representative,

116

N... and our governor, N.... Give them wisdom to lead well. Help us all to take our responsibilities as citizens seriously. Give us the courage to fight all discrimination, wherever we find it, so that our land truly can become one of "liberty and justice for all." And give us the strength and the willingness to work together for peace and justice throughout this world.

All: Amen.

If your family likes to sing, end with a patriotic song. If your family is not interested in a flag-raising ritual, still use the prayer as a blessing before the main meal of the day.

LABOR DAY

Labor Day signifies the end of the summer, the last picnic, the beginning of the work year for some people, and the school year for most children. It is a good day to consider the work that each member of the family does, both inside the home and out. This is a simple litany of praise to be prayed as a meal blessing or an opening for a family picnic.

Tell the family the leader of prayer will be mentioning several types of work that happen in the family: yard work, cleaning, cooking, schoolwork, doing dishes, and the like. Each time the leader mentions a type of work done in the family, everyone attempts to name all the people who contribute to that work. Some jobs may also involve people from outside the family.

After each job and its people are named, all respond "Let us bless the Lord."

All: Bless, O God, the work of our hands.

Leader: For those who care for our yard... (Everyone names people who help with yard work)

All: Let us bless the Lord.

Leader: For those who care for our cars...(names),
For those who cook the meals...
For those who do the dishes...
For those who keep the house clean...

117

> For those who learn in school...
> For those who make us all laugh...
> For those who give hugs and kisses so we
> know we are loved...
> For those who earn money for the family...

All: Let us bless the Lord.

Invite the family to chime in with any tasks you may have forgotten.

Leader: Lord, let our work be a source of joy for our family and a song of praise to you. We ask this in the name of Jesus, our Lord and brother.

All: Amen.

ALL SAINTS DAY

In the church, November 1 is the day when we remember all those saints who have no specific feast day, as well as all the saints who were never canonized by the church. These are the ordinary people who live good lives, lives of quiet holiness, ordinary people like you and me.

At supper on All Saints Day, invite your family to a canonization party. Decorate a cake or pudding with "Happy Feast Day to Us," and a candle for each member of the family. After dinner, before dessert, explain that in the church, people are declared saints by a process called canonization. In order to be canonized, there have to be three miracles attributed to the person in question. Their "cause" is then examined by a panel who decide if they should be formally canonized.

Point out to the family that there are "miracles" in all our lives. Getting through second grade may have been a real miracle for the child now doing well in fifth grade; treating someone who was cruel with real kindness may be another. The children themselves may be your miracles. Ask everyone to think of three miracles that have happened to them, or to someone else in the family. Keep the discussion lighthearted and fun.

Think of the people you would like to have on the panel to argue for your canonization. Who are the ones who think you are a holy, wonderful person? When you have decided that, ask everyone what they would like to have in a stained glass window dedicated to them. St. Joseph is often shown with his tools, St. Francis of Assisi with animals. What would each person's window look like?

Begin this All Saints Day ritual by taking out your Bible and having a family member read St. Paul's letter to the Colossians (3:12–15):

Reader: As God's chosen ones, holy and beloved, clothe yourselves with compassion, kindness, humility, meekness, and patience. Bear with one another and, if anyone has a complaint against another, forgive each other; just as the Lord has forgiven you, so you also must forgive. Above all, clothe yourselves with love, which binds everything together in perfect harmony. And let the peace of Christ rule in your hearts, to which indeed you were called in the one body. And be thankful.

Leader: Lord, you have called us to be saints. Bless us and help us to make our lives holy.

The leader then says the name of each member of the family (St. N...); after each all respond, "Pray for us."

Leader: All you saints and holy people of God,

All: Bless the Lord.

Light candles and sing "Happy Feast Day to Us," to the tune of "Happy Birthday."

THANKSGIVING

Thanksgiving falls appropriately at the end of our liturgical year. Christians can see this day as a time to give thanks for the old year and to prepare for the new one. Ask everyone to give a little thought in advance to the things they are grateful for this year. Then, as the "new year" will be starting with the first Sunday of Advent, ask them to begin to think about their resolutions.

The following ritual is most appropriate around the dinner table before the meal. The bread for the meal should be on the table.

Leader: Bless the Lord my soul, and remember all God's kindness. For the gift of... (name one gift of the past year for which you are thankful),

All: Bless the Lord, my soul.

Person to the right of the leader picks up the litany, then continue around the table until all have spoken.

Speaker: For the gift of...,

All: Bless the Lord, my soul.

Leader: The Lord's love lasts from all eternity, like God's goodness to our children's children. May we be ever aware of that love and grateful for God's goodness.

One child holds up the bread while another pronounces the blessing....

Child: Lord, bless the food you have provided for us, bless those who worked for it, those who prepared it, and those who gather to share it in love.

All: Amen.

Read Psalm 103, if you wish to make the prayer more formal.

PART IV

RITUALS

FROM

TRADITION

The Catholic faith is rich in traditional rituals. At one time in our church, these traditions were so strongly stressed that contemplative prayer was all but overlooked. The Second Vatican Council and the various renewal movements in the church of the 1960s and 1970s brought a healthy rebirth of interest in contemplation and spontaneous prayer. At the same time, however, traditional ritual has been de-emphasized. Both have a place in true Catholic spirituality.

Some of the more common Catholic traditions are included here. You may find there are one or two that fit your prayer life, your lifestyle, and that of your family. Include them in the events that you celebrate with your children.

THE ROSARY

The rosary is a traditional prayer to honor Mary. Rosary means "garland of roses." It is a garland of prayer to Mary. The rosary has a cross, followed by one large bead and three small ones and one more large bead. Then there is a circle with five decades. Each decade is made up of one large bead followed by ten smaller beads.

In praying the rosary, Hail Marys are repeated over and over as we reflect on special events in the life of Jesus and Mary. These events are called mysteries: the five Joyful Mysteries; the five Sorrowful Mysteries; and the five Glorious Mysteries. In saying the rosary, tradition says that we reflect on the Joyful Mysteries on Monday and Thursday, the Sorrowful on Tuesday and Friday, and the Glorious on Wednesday, Saturday, and Sunday. However, I have often found that certain mysteries have been more suited to certain times in my life, or to the person for whom I was praying.

The rosary is prayed in the following manner. Begin with a sign of the cross and the Apostles' Creed, recited while holding the crucifix. The Our Father is said on the first large bead, three Hail Marys on the three smaller ones, the Glory Be on the larger bead. The first mystery is then called to mind. The Our Father is recited, then ten Hail Marys on the ten smaller beads and a Glory Be on the large bead. The second mystery is called to mind, the Our Father recited, and so on through the five decades. End with the prayer Hail, Holy Queen.

The Joyful Mysteries
These tell of the events during the early life of Jesus.
1. The Annunciation (the angel Gabriel comes to Mary)
2. The Visitation (Mary visits her cousin Elizabeth)
3. The Birth of Jesus
4. The Presentation of Jesus in the Temple
5. The Finding of the Child Jesus in the Temple

The Sorrowful Mysteries
These tell of Jesus' passion and death.
1. The Agony of Jesus in the Garden
2. The Scourging at the Pillar
3. The Crowning with Thorns
4. The Carrying of the Cross
5. The Crucifixion and Death of Jesus

The Glorious Mysteries
These tell of the events that followed Jesus' resurrection.
1. The Resurrection of Jesus
2. The Ascension of Jesus into Heaven
3. The Descent of the Holy Spirit on the Apostles (Pentecost)
4. The Assumption of Mary into Heaven
5. The Crowning of Mary as Queen of Heaven

HAIL, HOLY QUEEN

Hail, holy Queen, mother of mercy, our life, our sweetness and our hope. To you do we cry, poor banished children of Eve; to you do we send up our sighs, mourning and weeping in this valley of tears. Turn, then, most gracious advocate, your eyes of mercy toward us; and after this, our exile, show unto us the blessed fruit of your womb, Jesus. O clement, O loving, O sweet Virgin Mary.

Verse: Pray for us, O holy Mother of God,
Response: That we may be made worthy of the promises of Christ.

THE ANGELUS

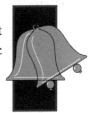

The Angelus is another traditional prayer in honor of Mary. It is recited early in the morning, at noon, and at dusk. In Catholic countries, such as Ireland, church bells often rang at the time of the Angelus. This prayer is usually recited with a leader and a response, although it can certainly be said by one person.

Leader: The angel of the Lord declared unto Mary,

Response: And she conceived of the Holy Spirit.

Leader: Hail Mary, full of grace, the Lord is with you. Blessed are you among women and blessed is the fruit of your womb, Jesus.

Response: Holy Mary, Mother of God, pray for us sinners, now and at the hour of our death. Amen.

Leader: Behold the handmaiden of the Lord.

Response: Be it done unto me according to your word.

Leader: Hail Mary…(as above),

Response: Holy Mary… (as above).

Leader: And the Word was made flesh

Response: And dwelt among us.

Leader: Hail Mary…

Response: Holy Mary…

Leader: Pray for us, holy Mother of God,

Response: That we may be made worthy of the promises of Christ.

Leader: Let us pray…

All: Pour forth, we beseech you, O Lord, your grace into our hearts, that we to whom the incarnation of Christ, your Son, was made known by the message of an angel, may, by his passion and cross, be brought to the glory of his resurrection, through the same Christ, our Lord. Amen.

NOVENA

Novena comes from the Latin word for nine and refers to nine days of prayers. It has been a tradition in the church for several centuries to pray to a particular saint, to Mary, or to Jesus, for a special intention for nine consecutive days, repeating the same prayer nine times. Have you ever seen a thank you to St. Jude, the patron saint of hopeless cases, posted in the newspaper? Many people believe that when you make a novena to St. Jude you are to thank the saint publicly when your prayer is answered.

There are books of novenas available at most Catholic bookstores, or you can simply make up your own prayer to a favorite saint and say it faithfully for nine days. My favorite novena from childhood was to the child Jesus. One would kneel before the Blessed Sacrament, the statue of the Infant of Prague, or an image of the child Jesus, and pray the "Glory Be" twelve times, with hands cupped open to receive the many blessings God showered down on you. There was something about the physical motion of cupping my hands and picturing God answering my prayer that made this a very satisfying novena for me as a child.

Since children love ritual and repetition, novenas answer the need for repetition with a fairly simple format. Novenas can be an uncomplicated way for the family to pray together in times of serious need.

THE WAY (STATIONS) OF THE CROSS

The Way of the Cross follows Jesus on his way to Calvary. There are fourteen stations, or stops along the route. They are depicted in churches by small carvings, pictures, or crosses along the wall of the church. The person(s) praying the stations goes from one to the next, remembering at each the passion and death of Jesus, and reflecting on some particular aspect of his suffering. There are many booklets available for praying the Way of the Cross, or it can be prayed by simply walking from station to station and reflecting on that moment in the passion of the Lord.

This is a Way of the Cross for parents. It can be prayed as is, or you may want to add an Our Father, Hail Mary, and Glory Be (or any one of those prayers) at the end of each reflection. You can use this in church, or for personal reflection in your home.

The First Station: Jesus is condemned to die.

Leader: We adore you, O Christ, and we bless you...

Response: Because by your holy cross you have redeemed the world.

The above verse and response are commonly said at each station, and it is traditional to genuflect while saying them.

Prayer: Lord, you were condemned, even though you were innocent. How easy it is for us to condemn our children based on appearances. Help us to listen and to search for truth.

The Second Station: Jesus receives his cross.

Leader: We adore you, O Christ...

Response: Because by your holy cross...

Prayer: Lord, weighed down under your cross, remind us that our children too carry crosses. They may not seem weighty to us, but they can be monumental to them. Help us to recognize the crosses in their lives and to teach them how to accept them.

The Third Station: Jesus falls the first time.

We adore you, O Christ...

Prayer: Lord, you fell under your cross. Help us to understand that failure is part of the journey. Enable us to accept failure in our children, and to help them up again.

The Fourth Station: Jesus meets his mother.

We adore you, O Christ...

Prayer: Lord, that meeting must have been so painful. Help us to understand that our children may cause us pain in answering your call. Give us the strength always to greet them as Mary greeted you, with love and compassion.

The Fifth Station: Simon the Cyrene helps Jesus to carry his cross.
We adore you, O Christ...

Prayer: Lord, you are the son of God, and you could not carry your own cross. Help us not to expect more of our children than your Father expected of you.

The Sixth Station: Veronica wipes the face of Jesus.
We adore you, O Christ...

Prayer: Lord, Veronica stands there quietly, reminding us of the need for gentle compassion and caring in another's suffering. No words could have expressed love better than the cloth that wiped your face. Help us to be silent when we feel compelled to advise, help us to offer what is truly needed.

The Seventh Station: Jesus falls the second time.
We adore you, O Christ...

Prayer: Lord, not only do our children fail, we fail them as parents, again and again. You remind all of us of the importance of getting back up each time we fall.

The Eighth Station: The women of Jerusalem weep over Jesus.
We adore you, O Christ...

Prayer: Lord, the women of Jerusalem remind me of the terrible responsibility of parenthood. Every child who suffers becomes my child; as a parent, it becomes my duty to reach out and ease that pain.

The Ninth Station: Jesus falls the third time.
We adore you, O Christ...

Prayer: Lord, not only do we fail as individuals, we fail as family. We fail to be light to the world and salt to the earth, a living witness to your love by our love for one another. As you got up and went on toward Calvary, teach us to get up and to try again.

The Tenth Station: Jesus is stripped of his garments.

We adore you, O Christ...

Prayer: Lord, I know what it is to be stripped. Our family knows us as no one else will ever know us. Family strips us of all our pretenses, and calls us to be real. Teach me to let go willingly. Help me to teach my children to let go.

The Eleventh Station: Jesus is nailed to the cross.

We adore you, O Christ...

Prayer: Lord, parenting, for all its joys, is like being nailed to a cross. We cannot set it aside for a moment. There is no escape from it. Once we have chosen it, it is ours until we die on it. Help me to open my arms wide to receive the cross I have chosen.

The Twelfth Station: Jesus dies on the cross.

We adore you, O Christ...

Prayer: Lord, I am not only crucified with you, but as a parent, I also stand beneath the cross with Mary and watch my child die. As a parent, it is a far greater death to watch your child suffer. Let me remember to turn to your mother in those moments of darkness.

The Thirteenth Station: Jesus is taken down from the cross.

We adore you, O Christ...

Prayer: Lord, help us to receive all the brokenness, all the dying of our children, with the open arms of your mother. Help us to be there for them even when there is nothing left to do except hold them.

The Fourteenth Station: Jesus is laid in the tomb.

We adore you, O Christ...

Prayer: Lord, there is a time when we must entrust our children totally into your hands. Help us to remember, in those desperate moments, that you love them more than we could ever imagine.

Although tradition only celebrates fourteen stations, I believe a fifteenth is needed: the empty tomb. Jesus rose from the dead, and in all our dying he is present, calling us to new life. If you are in church, stop a moment before the altar or baptismal font and reflect on the new life you see in your children. Thank God for the new life their presence has brought into your life.

LITANY

One of the traditional forms of prayer in our church is the litany. Litanies can be prayers of petition or prayers of praise. The "Labor Day" ritual and "Summer Vacation" ritual offer examples of litanies of praise. The "All Saints Day" ritual offers a simple litany of petition.

A litany is basically a call and response prayer. Use this format to create litanies that are appropriate for your family's needs and situations.

Leader: Lord, have mercy...

Response: Christ, have mercy.

Leader: Lord, have mercy, Christ hear us.

Response: Christ graciously hear us.

Leader: God, the Father of heaven,

Response: Have mercy on us.

Leader: God, the Son, redeemer of the world,

Response: Have mercy on us.

Leader: God, the Holy Spirit,

Response: Have mercy on us.

Leader: Holy Trinity, one God,

Response: Have mercy on us.

Leader: Holy Mary,

Response: Pray for us.

After the leader reads each of these petitions, all respond "pray for us."

Mary, daughter of Anne and Joachim...
Mary, gentle Jew...
Mary, unwed, pregnant teenager...
Mary, caring for an elderly aunt...
Mary, giving birth far from home...
Mary, fleeing to protect your child...
Mary, wife of a carpenter...
Mary, aunt of the prophet John...
Mary, mother who taught Jesus to walk...
Mary, mother who answered his cries...
Mary, mother who washed his clothes...
Mary, mother who fixed his meals...
Mary, mother who taught Jesus to pray...
Mary, mother of a gifted child...
Mary, mother of a rebellious preteen...
Mary, mother of a single adult...
Mary, mother of a self-taught rabbi...
Mary, mother of a wanderer...
Mary, mother of a healer...
Mary, mother of a religious rebel...
Mary, mother of a visionary...
Mary, mother of a convicted felon...
Mary, mother of a crucified son...
Mary, mother of the risen Lord...
Mary, mother of the church...
Mary, mother of God...

Leader: Let us pray...

Mary, you lived your life as wife and mother. You knew the monotony of daily chores, the delight in first steps and first words, the anguish of a missing child, the fears and hopes, concerns and joys shared by all families. Help us to recognize in the simplicity of your life, the holiness of our own. Pray with us, that we, too, might be a holy family. We ask this in the name of Jesus, your Son. Amen.

SUGGESTED RESOURCES

The books included in this list represent texts that may be helpful to you in praying as family, in planning family celebrations, and in developing family traditions.

Berg, Elizabeth. *Reader's Digest Good Times: New and Traditional Celebrations for the Whole Family.* Pleasantville, NY: Reader's Digest Association, 1992.

DeGidio, Sandra. *Enriching Faith through Family Celebrations.* Mystic, CT: Twenty-Third Publications, 1989.

Earth Works Group. *Fifty Simple Things You Can Do to Save the Earth.* Pasadena, CA: Greenleaf Publications, 1990.

Farry, Ginger. *Through Family Times: A Conversational Prayerbook for Today's World.* Mahwah, NJ: Paulist Press, 1993.

Fox, Robert J. *A Catholic Prayer Book.* Huntington, IN: Our Sunday Visitor, Inc., 1974.

Frost, Gerhard E. *Blessed Is the Ordinary.* Minneapolis, MN: Winston, 1980.

Hays, Edward. *Prayers for the Domestic Church: A Handbook for Worship in the Home.* Leavenworth, KS: Forest of Peace Books, Inc., 1989.

Meehan, Bridget Mary. *Prayers, Activities, Celebrations, (and More) for Catholic Families.* Mystic, CT: Twenty-Third Publications, 1995.

National Conference of Catholic Bishops. *Catholic Household Blessings and Prayers.* Washington, DC: United States Catholic Conference, 1989.

Office of Religious Education of the Diocese of Wilmington. *Keepers of the Promise: A Parent's Guide to Handing on Faith, Vol. I, II, III.* Wilmington, DE: Office of Religious Education, 1994.

Roberto, John. *Family Celebrations and Rituals.* New Rochelle, NY: Don Bosco Multimedia, 1992.

Travnikar, Rock. *The Blessing Cup: Forty Simple Rites for Family Prayer Celebrations.* Cincinnati, OH: St. Anthony Messenger Press, 1993.

Twenty-Third Publications in Mystic, CT has an extensive line of Way of the Cross booklets that are useful for the home. Here are some of them.

Jones, Sue. *The Way of the Cross for Parents.* 1995.

McCann, Deborah. *A Mother's Way of the Cross.* 1990.

Abajian, Diane. *Praying and Doing the Stations of the Cross with Children.* 1980. (Ages 4-7)

Costello, Gwen. *A Bible Way of the Cross for Children.* 1987. (Ages 7-12)

Costello, Gwen. *Stations of the Cross for Teenagers.* 1988. (Ages 12-18)

Huebsch, Bill. *The New Scripture Way of the Cross.* 1992.

Of Related Interest...

Prayers, Activities, Celebrations (and More) for Catholic Families
Bridget Mary Meehan

This book provides ideas and inspiration that help parents recognize the love of the Lord in routine events and relationships. At the same time, it shows how to refocus the family in terms of faith development.

ISBN: 0-89622-641-7, 96 pp, $7.95

Thinking About God
Susan McCaslin
Illustrated by Dorry Clay

Typical questions from a child—*Mommy, can you see God?*—are the basis for a simple and charming dialogue between a mother and child in this book. The answers are thoughtful, straightforward and uninhibited.

ISBN: 0-89622-615-8, 24 pp, Cloth, $7.95

Catholic Customs and Traditions
A Popular Guide
Greg Dues

How did the rosary originate? What meaning do certain colors have in Catholic worship? Why are oils important? These and other practices are explained in this revised and expanded edition.

ISBN: 0-89622-515-1, 221 pp, $9.95

Available at religious bookstores or from

TWENTY-THIRD PUBLICATIONS
P.O. Box 180 • Mystic, CT 06355

1-800-321-0411